ILLUMINATED MANUSCRIPTS

Richard Hayman

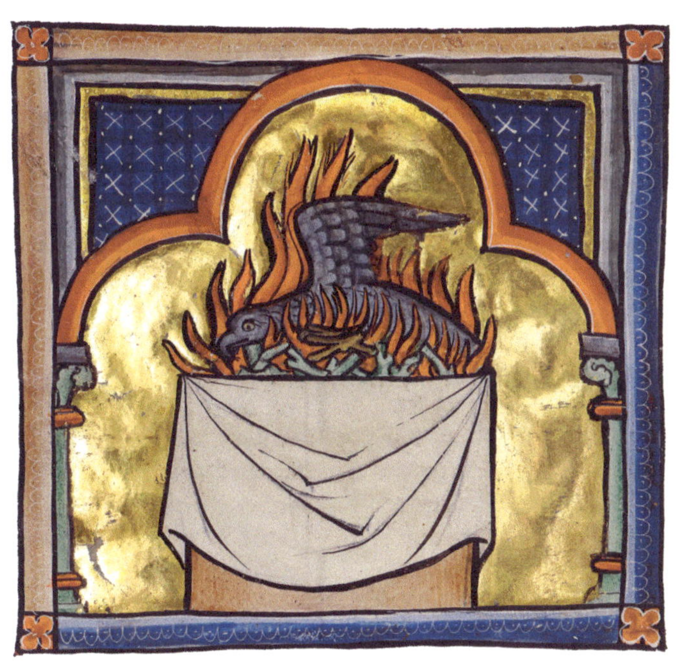

SHIRE PUBLICATIONS
Bloomsbury Publishing Plc

Kemp House, Chawley Park, Oxford OX2 9PH, UK
Bloomsbury Publishing Ireland Limited,
29 Earlsfort Terrace, Dublin 2, D02 AY28, Ireland
1385 Broadway, 5th Floor, New York, NY 10018, USA
Email: shire@bloomsbury.com
www.shirebooks.co.uk

SHIRE is a trademark of Osprey Publishing Ltd
First published in Great Britain in 2017
Transferred to digital print in 2023

© Richard Hayman, 2017

Richard Hayman has asserted his right under the
Copyright, Designs and Patents Act, 1988, to be
identified as the author of this book.

All rights reserved. No part of this publication may be:
i) reproduced or transmitted in any form, electronic
or mechanical, including photocopying, recording
or by means of any information storage or retrieval
system without prior permission in writing from the
publishers; or ii) used or reproduced in any way for
the training, development or operation of artificial
intelligence (AI) technologies, including generative AI
technologies. The rights holders expressly reserve this
publication from the text and data mining exception
as per Article 4(3) of the Digital Single Market
Directive (EU) 2019/790.

A catalogue record for this book is available from
the British Library.

Shire Library no. 841
Print ISBN: 9781784422363 – ePub: 9781784422356
ePDF: 9781784422370 – XML: 9781784422387

Typeset in Garamond Pro and Gill Sans
Page layouts by PDQ Digital Media Solutions, UK
Printed and bound in Great Britain by CPI (Group)
UK Ltd, Croydon CR0 4YY

25 26 27 28 29   12 11 10 9 8 7

Product safety
For product safety related questions contact:
productsafety@bloomsbury.com

The Woodland Trust
Shire Publications supports the Woodland Trust,
the UK's leading woodland conservation charity.

www.shirebooks.co.uk
To find out more about our authors and books visit our
website. Here you will find extracts, author interviews,
details of forthcoming events and the option to sign-up
for our newsletter.

COVER IMAGE
A miniature of St Catherine of Alexandria being
tended by angels during her imprisonment for refusing
to worship pagan idols, by the Spitz Master, France,
*c.*1420. (J. Paul Getty Museum, Digital image courtesy
of the Getty's Open Content Program) Back cover
image: An elaborate 'B' from the start of Psalm 1 in the
Arundel Psalter, produced in Canterbury between 1012
and 1023. (British Library Public Domain image)

TITLE PAGE IMAGE
A phoenix had the power to set itself alight in old age
so that a new bird could arise from the ashes. For the
medieval reader it was a reminder that Jesus sacrificed
himself to God but rose again.

CONTENTS PAGE IMAGE
The Whore of Babylon is revealed to St John by an
angel. She is riding on a beast, drunk with the blood
of the saints and holding a cup 'filled with abominable
things and the filth of her adulteries'. It is taken from
an English Apocalypse of the 1250s.

ACKNOWLEDGEMENTS
Copyright holders and permission to reproduce
illustrations has been given by:

Bavarian State Library, 8, 23, 24 (top), 54; Bibliothèque
Nationale de France (Public Domain), 53; British
Library, 14, 17, 31, 36, 50 (top); J. Paul Getty
Museum, (digital image courtesy of the Getty's Open
Content Program), pages 1, 3, 6, 7 (both), 12, 15
(left), 29 (both), 30, 41 (bottom), 42, 47, 49 (bottom),
50 (bottom), 51, 59, 63; The Chapter of Lichfield
Cathedral, 20; Metropolitan Museum of Art, 4, 19
(bottom), 24 (bottom), 32, 33, 39 (both), 40; National
Library of Sweden, 25; New York Public Library,
34; Southern Methodist University, 43; Staats- und
Universitätsbibliothek Bremen, 11; The Board of Trinity
College, Dublin, 22; Walters Art Gallery, 10, 13, 15
(right), 16 (both), 18 (both), 19 (top), 26, 27, 28, 35, 37
(both), 38, 41 (top), 44, 45, 46, 48 (both), 49 (top), 60.

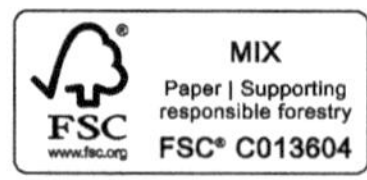

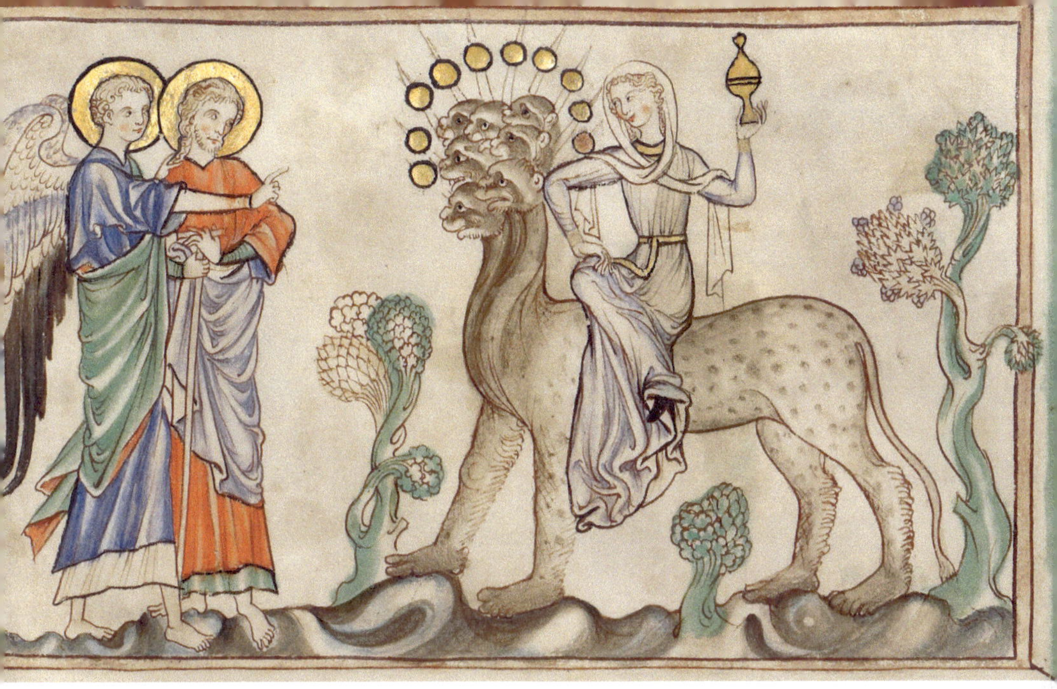

CONTENTS

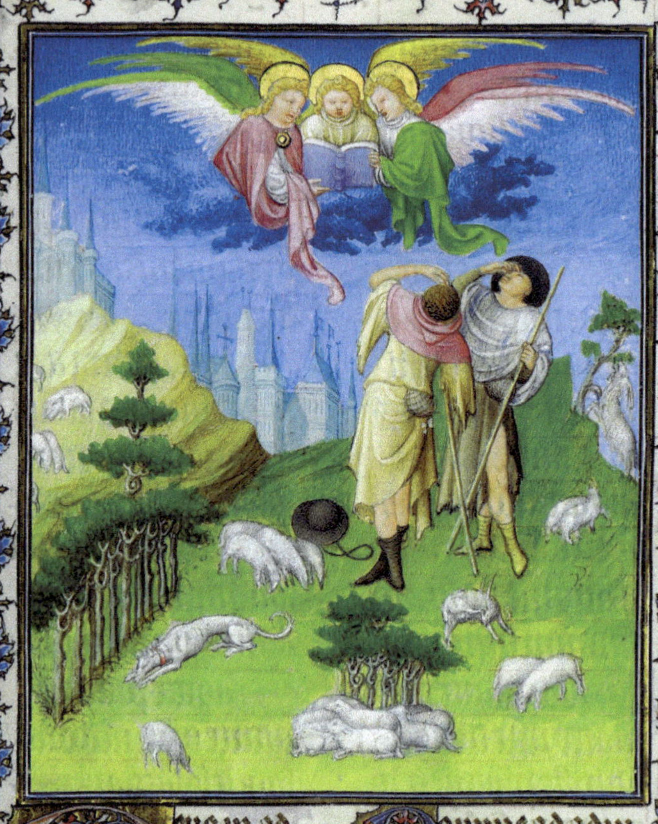

eus in ad
iutorium
meum in
tende.
Domine ad adiu
uandum me festina.
Gloria patri et filio
et spiritui sancto.

THE GLORIFICATION OF GOD

Illuminated manuscripts are the great secret history of the Middle Ages. The masterpieces of the period, ranging from the Book of Kells produced by Irish monks on Iona in the eighth century to the sumptuous *Les Très Riches Heures* made for the Duc de Berry in the fifteenth century, rank with the cathedrals of Europe as major cultural landmarks of the Middle Ages. They have been enjoyed in facsimile editions and exhibitions have displayed single pages in glass cabinets, but few people have ever had the privilege of turning the pages of an original illuminated manuscript. In a world where art is essentially a public affair, illuminated books were private, intimate works that were mainly experienced in silence and solitude. Medieval illuminated manuscripts have always had the connotation of hidden treasure and have retained a special mystique.

Manuscript means 'written by hand' and covers every type of book produced in the Middle Ages before the invention of the printing press. The illustrations became known as illuminations because gold and silver leaf combined with bright pigments to produce a rich shimmering effect on the page. In fact, some manuscripts were so richly illuminated with gold leaf that they were known as a Codex Aureus, a 'golden book'. Illuminated manuscripts are characteristic of a period that was rich in visual expression. The page was adorned with decorative, narrative and devotional images just as sculptures peopled the external walls of churches and painting adorned the interior.

Les Belles Heures, commissioned by the Duc de Berry and completed in 1409, is one of the most beautiful objects to have been created in the Middle Ages.

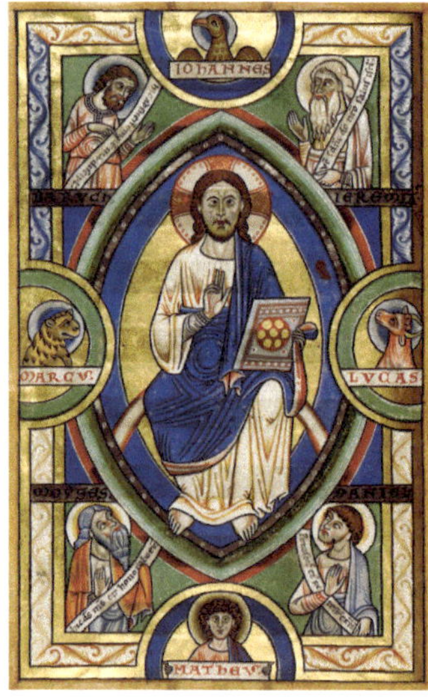

Christ in Majesty, surrounded by the four Evangelists and Old Testament prophets and patriarchs, is an illumination in gold leaf and tempera from a German Missal, or book of the Mass, of the 1170s.

The range of books produced in the Middle Ages includes sacred texts as well as secular works such as histories, philosophical works and Arthurian romances. Dante's *Inferno* and Chaucer's *Canterbury Tales* both first appeared in manuscript form. The majority of books, however, were religious in content. Christianity is the religion of the book (in classical antiquity there was no equivalent sacred text to the Christian Bible). The Bible is the physical embodiment of God's word and in the Middle Ages was a sacred object in its own right. We have forgotten the extent to which objects were important in medieval belief – as relics made the existence of saints seem more real so a beautiful Bible or other devotional book affirmed the truth of God's message.

At least until the thirteenth century books were mainly produced and consumed by religious men and women. One of the reasons that book production eventually flourished beyond the monastic cloister was that lay people started to purchase and read books as an act of private devotion, an expression of popular piety that grew steadily throughout the Middle Ages and showed no sign of declining when the Reformation and Counter-Reformation came in the sixteenth century. Some of the most sumptuously illustrated books were made for wealthy lay patrons, including royalty. They were worldly status symbols although, as comparatively small and private objects, an example of inconspicuous consumption. The motive that inspired people to commission a book either for personal use or for donation to a church was devotion to God.

In classical antiquity a text was a script for reading aloud, and consumers of literature expected to hear the words as much as see them on the page. The emergence of illuminated manuscripts charts a transition to silent, private reading. When they are depicted in art, classical authors are shown dictating to scribes, but in the Christian era the authors of the Gospels are shown writing their own texts. Writing became a sacred act. The work of copying text was a labour of love, but it was also long and laborious. With a sigh of relief an East Anglian scribe added at the end of a book of psalms, 'The book is finished. Praise and glory be to Christ. Amen.' No less a sacred act was the work of the illuminator. The illustrations in a medieval book are not merely ornament. They amplify the holiness of the text and transform the word of God into an object of beauty. Every beautiful medieval illuminated manuscript was made to glorify God.

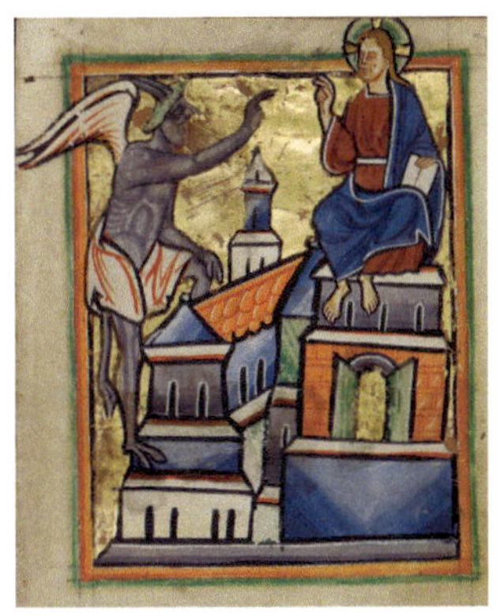

Satan tempts Christ to make a leap of faith from the top of the Temple in Jerusalem, a scene from St Matthew's Gospel illuminated with gold leaf in East Anglia c.1190.

The book has always been central to Christian worship and teaching, and the book form itself is closely associated with the rise of Christianity. Greek and Roman literature was written on one side of a roll of papyrus, but in the early Christian world it was superseded by the book, composed of many leaves bound together and written on both sides, known as a codex (plural codices). Codices illustrated with narrative scenes began to supersede the papyrus roll in the eastern Mediterranean by the fifth century. St Jerome (c.347–420), scholar and translator who lived much of his life in Syria and Constantinople, was critical of the new fashion for luxurious decoration of books, suggesting that it was a new phenomenon in his day. Ironically, many of the most beautiful books produced in the Middle Ages were of the Latin Bible, in a version known as the Vulgate which was translated by Jerome himself.

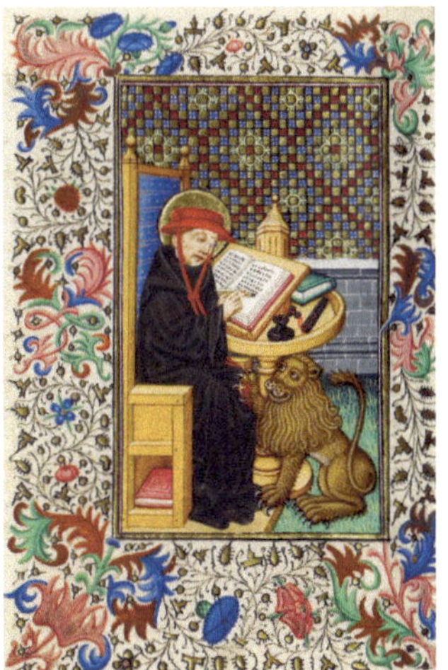

St Jerome is depicted in his study in a fifteenth-century Book of Hours by a French artist possibly working in London. Jerome's translation of the Bible, known as the Vulgate, was used throughout western Christendom in the Middle Ages.

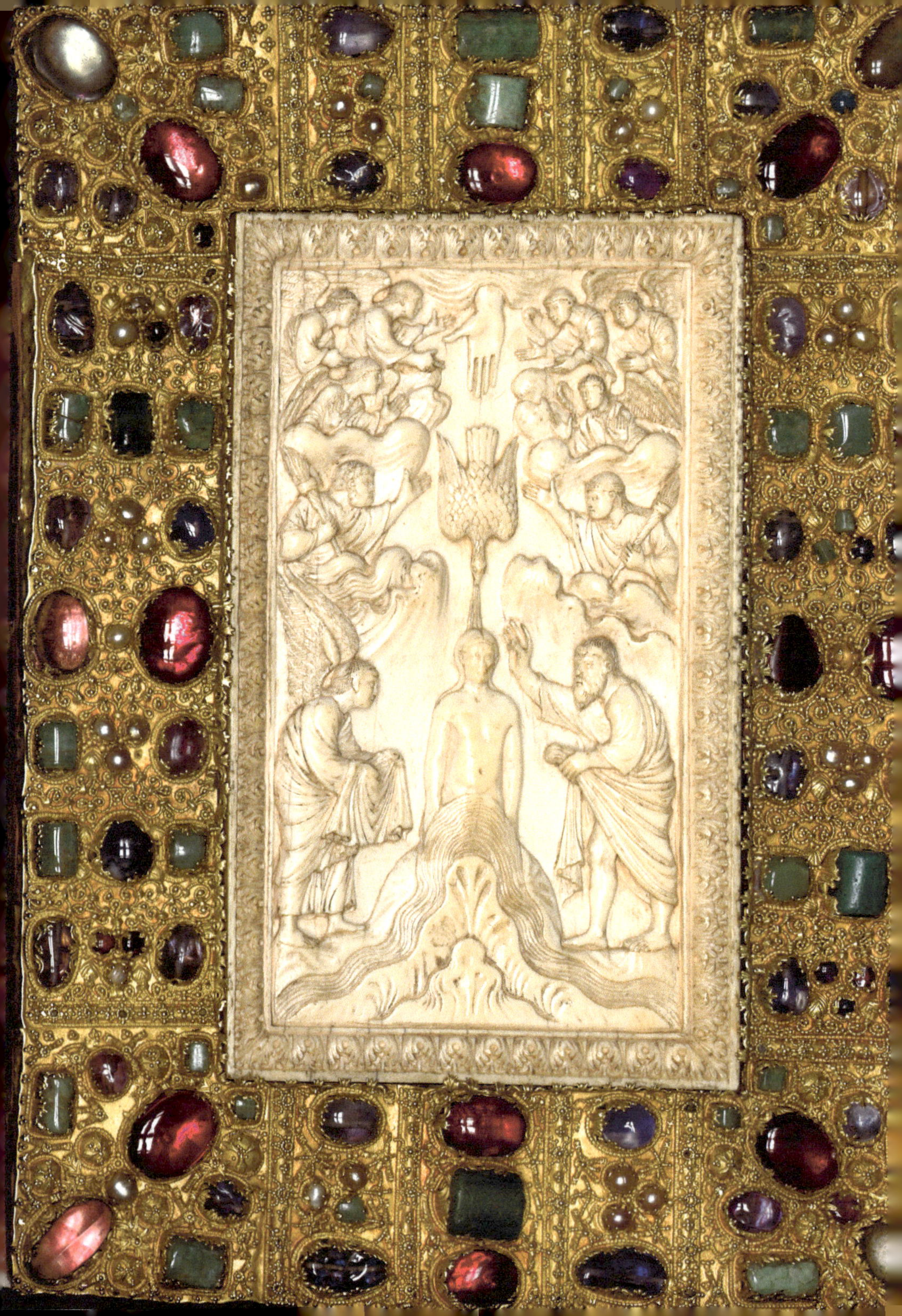

BOOK PRODUCTION

Illuminated manuscripts were produced on parchment, also known as vellum. Parchment was much more suitable than papyrus for a book in which pages were turned and, as it was made from the skins of animals, was more readily available across most of Europe than papyrus, which was invented by the Egyptians and was made from the stem of the papyrus plant found along the course of the Nile. Parchment was made from the skins of sheep or calves, so could never be mass-produced like paper. The skins were soaked, bathed in a lime solution, scraped, rinsed, stretched and cleaned with pumice and water, leaving a smooth surface ideal for the scribe and illuminator.

Parchment naturally forms oblong pieces and it has dictated the standard shape of the book ever since. Books, however, varied in size. For a large volume single pieces of vellum were folded in half and usually four folded pieces were placed inside each other to form eight leaves (the equivalent of sixteen pages), which were known as a 'quire' or gathering. For smaller books a single piece of vellum could be folded twice and trimmed, to produce four leaves, or folded again and trimmed to produce a quire of eight leaves. A book was composed of a series of quires bound in sequence. Few medieval books had numbered pages and the convention is to count leaves (known as folios) rather than pages, each of which has a front (recto) and back (verso).

Before a scribe could begin work, ruled lines and margins were drawn to ensure regularity of the text. The manuscript

The jewelled binding with pearls and precious stones set in a gold plate with filigree decoration, and including an inset ivory panel showing the baptism of Christ, shows the opulence of the most luxurious ninth-century Gospel Books made in Germany.

This page of Gothic script from a thirteenth-century Gospel Book produced in Oxford shows lines ruled in order to keep the text regular.

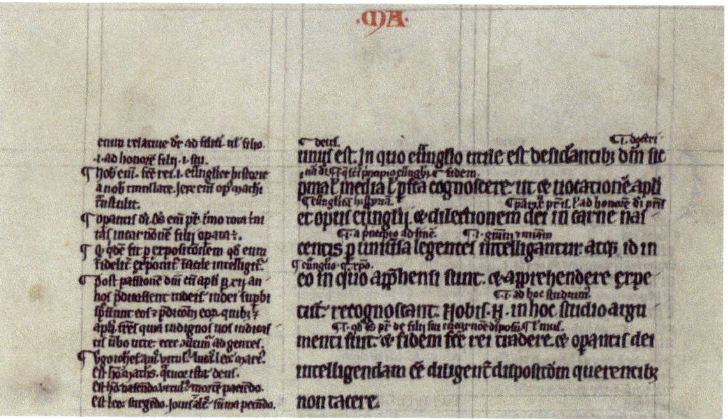

was placed on an angled rest and the scribe set to work with a quill made of goose feather, carefully copying out the words from an exemplar. Black and brown inks were the most commonly used, the former carbon-based from ground-up soot, the latter derived from oak galls. Red ink, made from red lead, was used to highlight instructions in liturgical books, from which we derive the terms 'rubric' and 'red-letter days'.

The text was completed before the manuscript was handed over to the illuminator, or limnour (a general word used for artists painting any kind of miniature). Tempera was the medium used in decorating medieval manuscripts, in which pigments are mixed with water, and with egg yolk or egg whites as a binding agent. It is well suited to the smooth surfaces of vellum. Pigments were derived mainly from a variety of coloured minerals, some of them imported from exotic places and testament to international trade from the early Middle Ages. Ultramarine, made up of ground lapis lazuli boiled with wax, oil and resin to create a deep-blue dye, was imported from Afghanistan. Various shades of blue were also obtained from copper carbonate. When copper is exposed to acid such as vinegar it becomes discoloured and creates a substance known as verdigris that can be scraped off and mixed with vinegar to make green paint. Bluish shades could be obtained from indigo and woad, also used by scribes, white was obtained from the ashes of bone, while cochineal (the crushed shells of dried insects) yielded a scarlet colour. The characteristics of the materials were well understood by the artists, who knew whether to mix or layer their colours for the best effects on the page.

The subject matter was first outlined in charcoal, with aids like compasses used to mark out circles. Gold was rare in illuminated manuscripts before the mid-twelfth century but, if it was to be used, it was applied before the colours. Gold leaf was laid on wet glue, such as gum ammoniac, and then burnished until it shone (a process that would have damaged painted areas had they been finished first).

When the decoration was complete the quires were gathered together and the book was bound, always on the left side. They were sewn into horizontal thongs of leather which were then threaded into grooves in the wooden board that made up the spine of the cover. Bindings were usually covered in leather or decorated fabric, but the original cover is the component of a medieval manuscript least likely to survive.

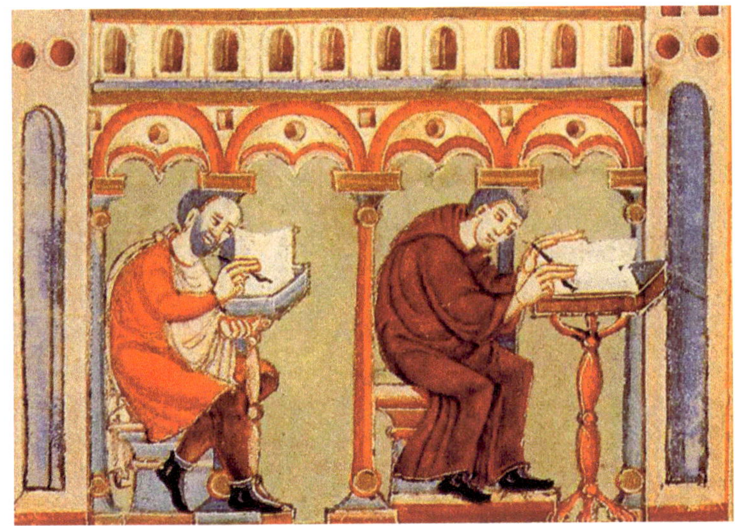

A lay brother and a monk work as scribes at lecterns in the cloisters of Echternach Abbey in Luxembourg, *c.*1040.

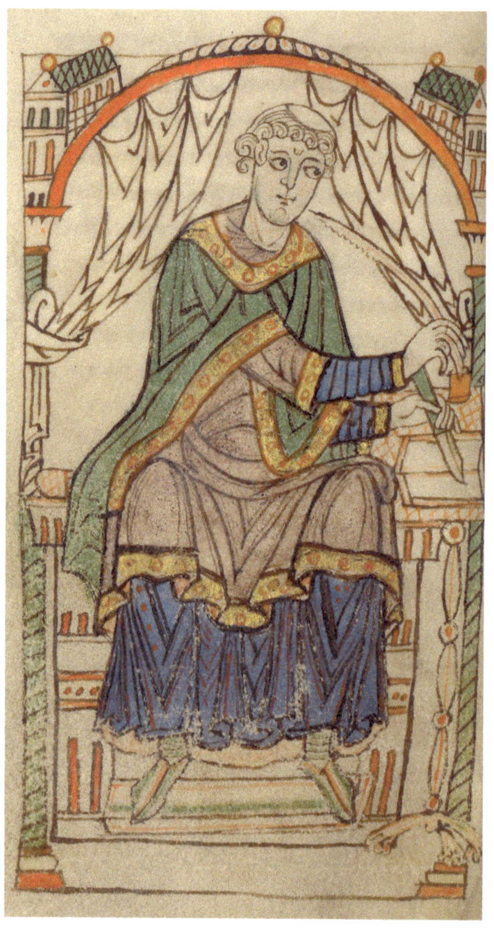

Eadmer of Canterbury (c.1060–1126) was the author of a biography of St Anselm, Archbishop of Canterbury, and is depicted in a twelfth-century illumination as a scribe.

Many manuscripts have been re-bound on several occasions. The most lavish books were bound in covers set with enamels, jewels and ivory carvings that made them valuable in more than just a spiritual sense. When Viking raiders stole the Codex Aureus from Canterbury in the ninth century, they were probably more interested in the value of the precious metal and minerals than they were in spiritual enlightenment. The thieves discarded the book itself, which was later recovered and is now in the National Library of Sweden. Likewise the Book of Kells, which in common with many Irish manuscripts of the time was enclosed in a lavish portable shrine, was stolen in 1007, but not for the manuscript leaves, which were recovered.

Artists and scribes did not compose works but copied them from existing manuscripts, or 'exemplars'. It is an artistic tradition quite different from the modern world where originality is prized above everything else. The earliest pictorial representations of scribes show them writing with books on their laps (different from the classical tradition in which the author dictated to a scribe), and various references suggest that the labour in the early Irish scriptoria was conducted in the open air. Later illustrations show the scribe or illuminator in the relative comfort of the monastic cloister, working at a desk and with the book at an angle.

In the early centuries of book production the scribes and artists were invariably monks working in monastic scriptoria. Few of them are known by name – monks were not expected to seek personal glory – but when their names did appear it was usually to ask for prayers or to ask God to look mercifully upon them. The means by which many artists and scribes are known is a colophon, which is an inscription recording information about the production of the book separate from the main text. A colophon in the Lindisfarne Gospels, for example, says that the book was written by Eadfrith, bishop of Lindisfarne between 698 and 721, and was bound by Billfrith, an anchorite (a type of hermit). Other scribes have been identified according to local traditions. These men include St Dunstan, tenth-century abbot of Glastonbury, and Abbots Spearhavoc of Abingdon and Mannig of Evesham in the mid-eleventh century. Whether or not these traditions are apocryphal, the association of bishops and abbots with writing indicates that labour in the scriptorium had a high status and holiness.

Women in holy orders also worked as scribes and illuminators, and some of them are known by name. Guda, a nun working in the Middle Rhine in Germany in the twelfth century, added a colophon to a book of homilies in her own hand: 'Guda, a sinful woman, copied and painted this book'. A Spanish nun called Ende illuminated the Gerona Apocalypse, and other nuns are referred to as illuminators, such as Edith of Wilton in the tenth century, who was also skilled at embroidery.

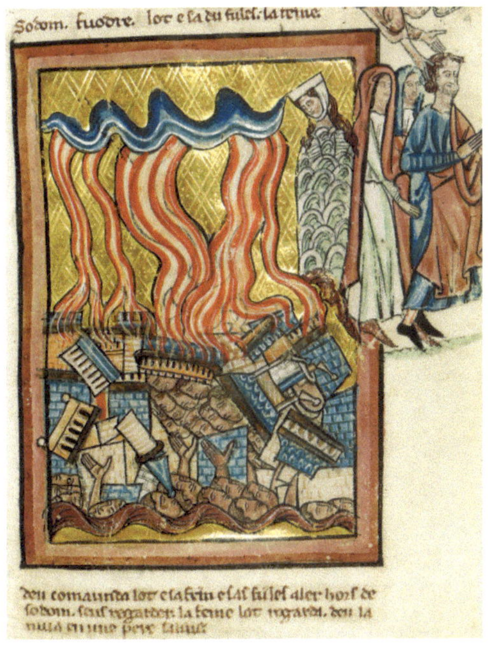

Lot and his family leave Sodom, a Bible miniature by William de Brailes, who was active in Oxford in the mid-thirteenth century and is one of the few English artists of the period known by name.

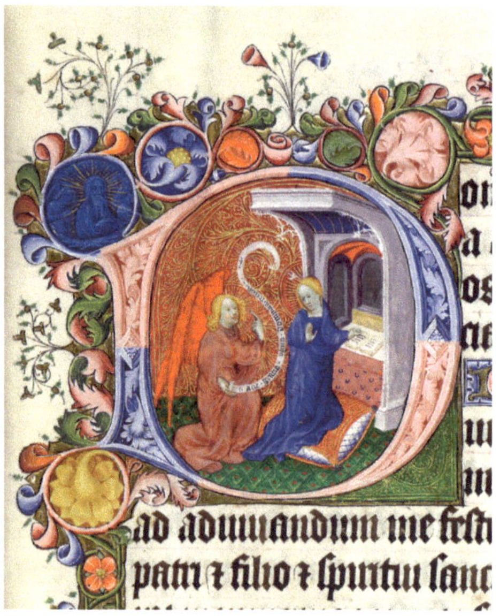

Herman Scheere was the illuminator of the Bedford Psalter, made for John Plantagenet, third son of Henry IV, in the early fifteenth century. This historiated initial depicts the Annunciation and is set in a rich foliate border.

The roles of scribe and illuminator soon became specialist skills. Ernwig, a monk at Peterborough and the tutor to St Wulfstan in the eleventh century, was skilled in both, but this was increasingly rare and some illuminators were probably brought into the monastery as lay brothers to work on manuscripts. There may have been an affinity between illuminators and goldsmiths. The illuminators used gold in their most precious paintings, and the more luxurious books were bound by goldsmiths. Two names mentioned in Canterbury in the twelfth century, the painter Albericus, and the goldsmith Albericus, may have been the same person.

All monasteries needed books and the great age of monastic book production in England began in the tenth century, gained fresh impetus after the Norman Conquest in 1066, and continued until the decline of new monastic foundations in the thirteenth century. By this time increasing numbers of books were produced by lay people working outside the monastery in workshops, or *ateliers*, in urban centres such as London and Oxford in England, and the major European cities. The finest artists in this period had varied backgrounds. Matthew Paris (*c.*1200–1259), a native Frenchman as his name implies, was a Benedictine monk at St Albans Abbey, and apart from his work as an illuminator was a noted chronicler. John Siferwas (*c.*1360–1430) trained as a Dominican friar and worked for monasteries in the south-west of England, including Glastonbury, where he produced a lectionary (a book of Bible extracts arranged for reading at religious services) for Salisbury Cathedral. Others were lay craftsmen.

William de Brailes, known to have been married and therefore not in holy orders, was working in Oxford in the mid-thirteenth century and was presumably from the village of Brailes in Warwickshire. Eleven manuscripts can be associated with him. By the fifteenth century the most noted limnours were not only secular artists, but travelled internationally. Herman and Johannes Scheere came originally from Germany, but Herman was working in London in the first quarter of the fifteenth century, and is identified by his motto '*Omnia levia sunt amanti: si quis amat non laborat*' ('all is easy for one who loves: he who loves toils not').

The appearance of manuscript pages changed considerably over the centuries in which they were produced. The early manuscripts of the British Isles are written in an Uncial script of rounded letters, derived from late classical prototypes.

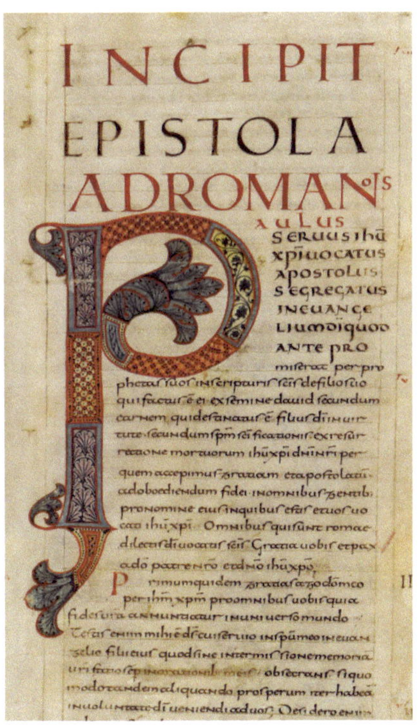

BELOW LEFT
This initial page and minuscule script is from the Epistle to the Romans, part of a ninth-century Gospel Book produced in Tours.

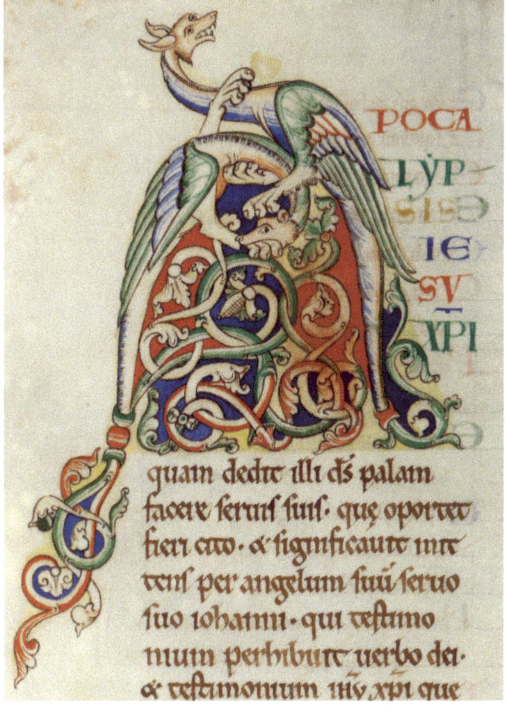

BELOW RIGHT
A pair of dragons forms an inhabited initial, from a twelfth-century manuscript created at Rochester Cathedral Priory.

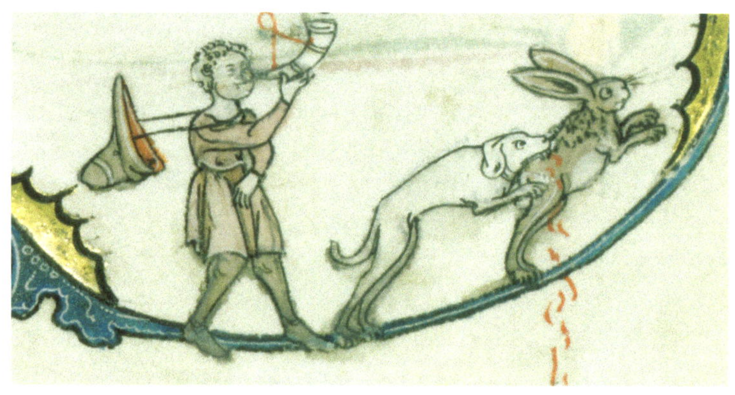

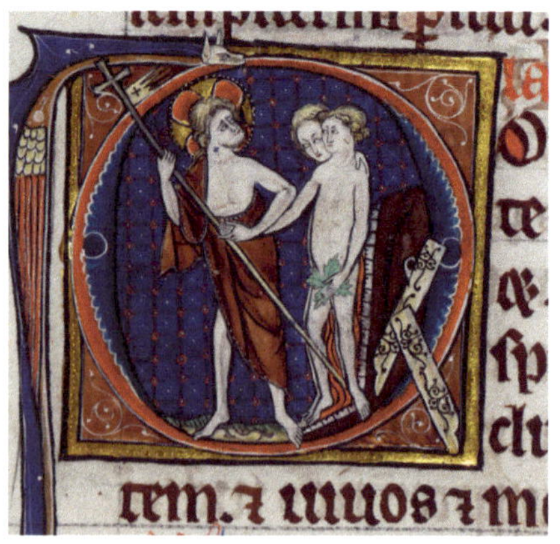

At the end of the eighth century, in the court of Charlemagne in the German town of Aachen, scribes developed a new, simpler form of script, known as Carolingian minuscule. The style enjoyed a revival in the Italian Renaissance, on the mistaken assumption that it was of Roman origin, and when printing began in Italy the printers adopted this 'Roman' type, which remains one of the most common typefaces in use today. In the twelfth century, however, forms of Gothic script with its elaborate, spiky appearance became popular and remained so throughout the Middle Ages – it was so ubiquitous that the first printed books in Germany and in England used a Gothic typeface.

Medieval manuscripts had no title pages, chapter headings or page numbers, without which large books such as the Bible are difficult to navigate. To overcome this, large decorated initials were used where a modern printed book would use chapter headings or sub-headings, and were the work of the illuminator rather than the scribe. Decorated initials became steadily more ambitious and became works of art in their own right. Where the initial incorporates a narrative scene, usually from the Bible, it is known as an historiated initial. Initials in which people appear as decorative devices are known as inhabited initials. Both types were common in medieval manuscripts.

Another way of highlighting important pages in a book was to decorate the margins of the text. Animals and plants feature strongly in marginal illuminations, which are in general stylised rather than studies in natural history as we would understand it. This could be purely decorative in intent, but as the roles of scribe and illuminator became specialised and separated, the illuminators began to use the margins to make visual annotations beside the text. Annotations were not new. The explanatory note, or 'gloss', was common in medieval manuscripts, whether squeezed between the main lines of text, or added outside the margins. The aim was to help readers understand difficult passages of the text, either because of their profundity or the difficulties of the Latin.

By the thirteenth century illuminators, usually now lay artisans rather than men in holy orders, offered more mischievous annotations. The Rutland Psalter, produced *c.* 1260 in England, is a notable early example of the art of marginalia, which includes depictions of humans, animals and imaginary beasts (taken from the Bestiary, which is described later) in

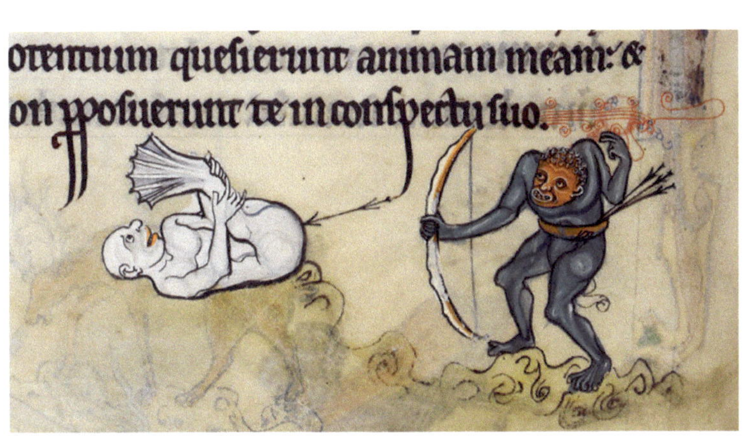

A page from the thirteenth-century Rutland Psalter has irreverent marginal decoration. Beneath the text an archer fires an arrow and scores a direct hit in the anus of a Sciapod, a mythical creature from the Bestiaries who used its large foot as a parasol to protect itself from the desert sun.

In this witty marginal decoration a man is seen pulling into place the missing fourth verse of Psalm 127, correcting the scribe's error, from an English Book of Hours of the late thirteenth century.

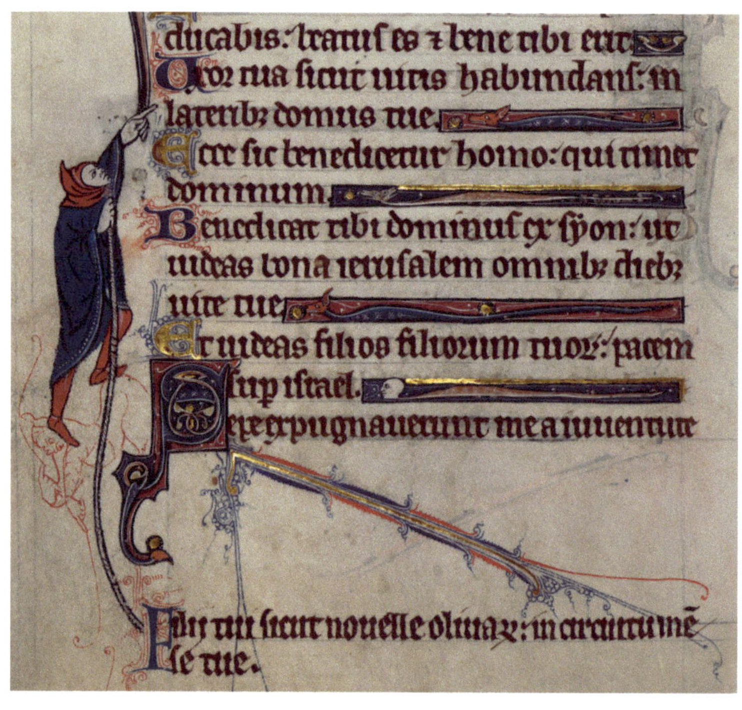

In the margin in this fourteenth-century Flemish Book of Hours is a woman at prayer, probably the owner who commissioned the book. Books of Hours were especially popular with women because of their focus on prayers in honour of the Virgin Mary.

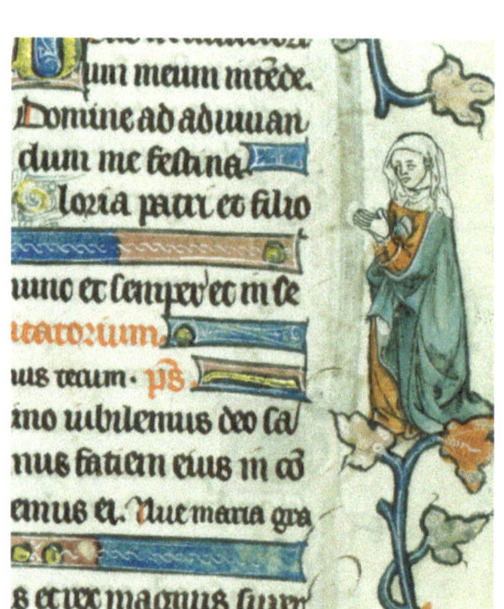

amusing and bawdy scenes. Irreverence characterises many of the marginal flourishes of medieval manuscripts, trying to raise a laugh from the reader of an otherwise solemn text. We can see illuminators indulging in visual puns, commenting on the work of scribes and depicting scenes from daily life which would have amused their patrons. Apes, kept as pets by the nobility, were often used to represent human folly. We can find them writing manuscripts, reading them, being suckled by nuns, playing music and so on.

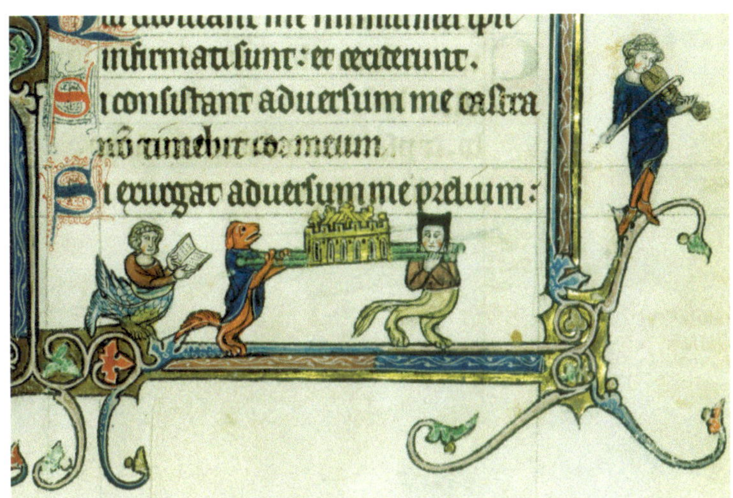

A dog and a hybrid man carry a reliquary, while a man plays a rebec and a hybrid man reads. These figures appear in the margin of a late-thirteenth-century Psalter.

The text and miniature of the Resurrection in this Flemish Book of Hours of c.1500 occupies only a small portion of the page, which is dominated by its rich border foliage.

The earliest illuminated manuscripts had illustrations on pages separate from the text, which are known as miniatures regardless of their size. Miniatures were later incorporated into the pages of text as well, especially prevalent with calendar scenes in the later Middle Ages. But in the most luxurious books, the miniatures occupied a full page. Even the earliest miniatures have decorative borders, as in the more lavish Irish Gospel Books which have borders with interlace decoration. In the fifteenth century the border became more prominent, especially in Books of Hours which were commissioned from lay artisans mainly for a lay audience. Books of Hours made in France and Flanders in the fifteenth century are characterised by the rich foliate borders in which the miniature painting itself takes up a relatively small proportion of the page. In these pages we can see the ultimate fulfilment of the medieval instinct for profuse decoration.

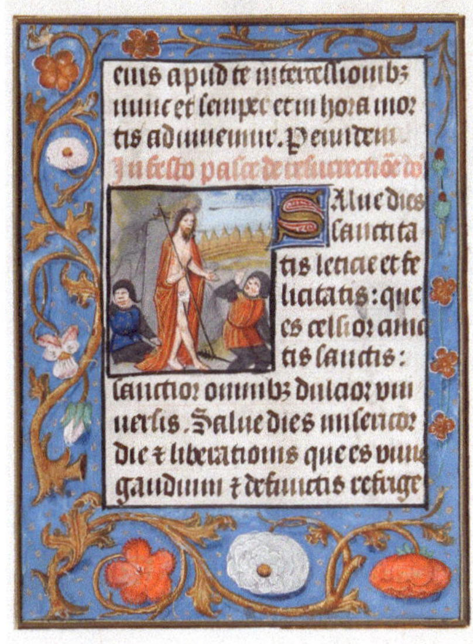

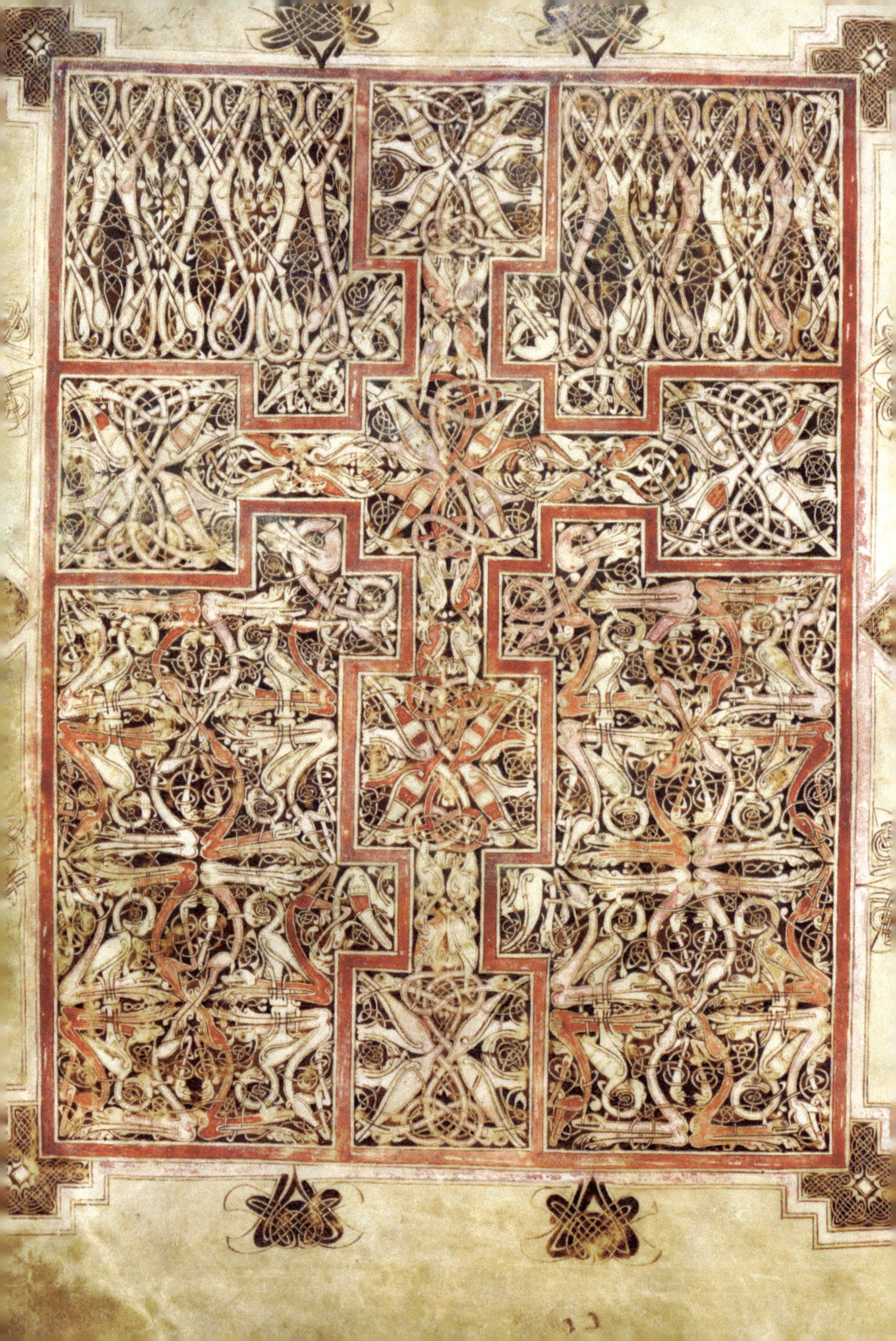

BOOKS AND THEIR ILLUMINATIONS

THE BIBLE

Early manuscript production was dominated by Bibles, or parts of Bibles. The Bible was the most important object possessed by any religious community – St John's Gospel opens 'In the beginning was the word and the word was God'. In practice a single-volume manuscript Bible (known as a pandect) was a very large book, and for practical reasons most of the early Biblical manuscripts are therefore sections of the Bible, principally the Gospels, but also Psalms and the Book of Revelation.

One of the oldest surviving Gospel Books, written in Old Latin and therefore pre-dating Jerome's Vulgate edition, is now in Cambridge University. It was produced in Italy in the late sixth century and seems likely to have been one of the books associated with the mission of Augustine, sent in AD 597 by Pope Gregory to convert the pagan English. Augustine founded a monastery at Canterbury that was soon an important centre of book production in its own right. The earliest surviving complete Vulgate edition of the Bible also has a strong British connection. It was produced at the twin monasteries of Monkwearmouth–Jarrow in Northumbria at the time when the Venerable Bede, England's first historian, was a monk there. This was a former Roman outpost region transformed into a centre of Christian culture. The book, now known as the Codex Amiatinus, is made up of 2,060 pages (or 1,030 folios), weighs 75kg and was written on the skins of

Carpet pages, pages with intricate decoration, are characteristic of Gospel Books produced in the British Isles in the eighth century. This example, in the form of a cross, is from the St Chad Gospels, probably produced in Wales.

The Virgin and Child (with two left feet) are attended by four angels and set in a frame of Celtic interlace decoration in the first full-page illumination in the Book of Kells.

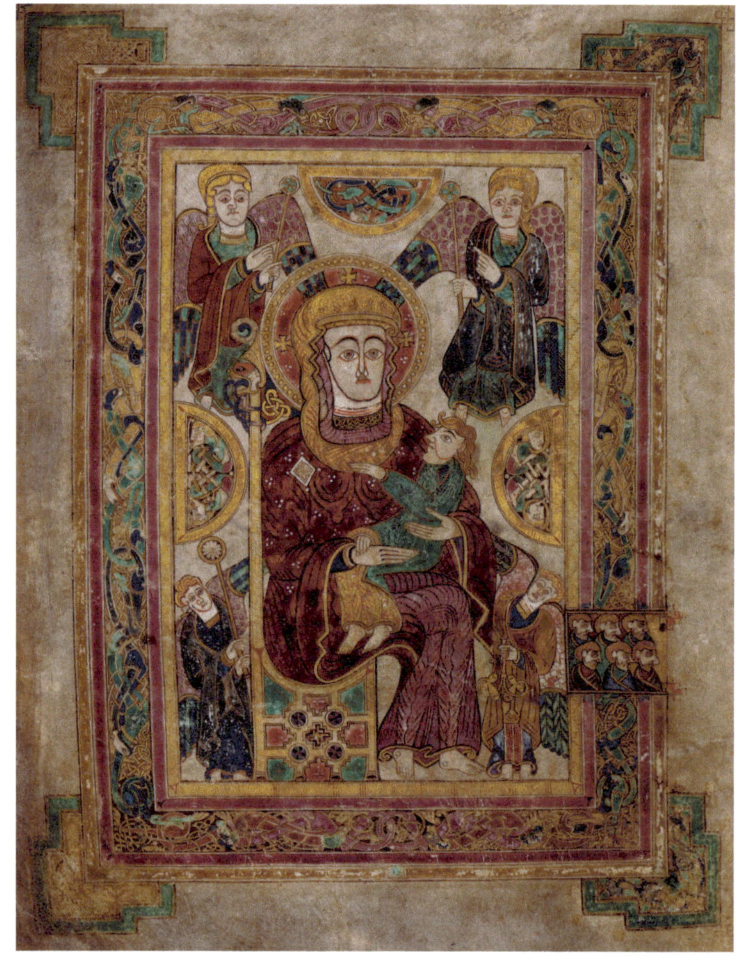

515 young calves. The Codex Amiatinus was one of a trio of Bibles produced at Monkwearmouth–Jarrow *c.*700, and was made for presentation to the Pope himself. Unfortunately the book's owners seem to have perished on their pilgrimage to Rome, but the book survived and has been in Italy ever since.

The most remarkable group of early medieval Gospel Books was produced in the British Isles, beginning in the seventh century. Gospel Books produced by the Irish scriptoria, most famously the community of Irish monks founded by Colum Cille (or St Columba, 521–597) on Iona, include the Books of Durrow and Kells. Ionian influence was to spread to Lindisfarne off the Northumbrian coast, where the Lindisfarne Gospels were produced *c*.700. These texts belong to what is known misleadingly as the 'Insular style', intending to mean 'from the islands' rather than inward looking. They are among the finest works of art of early medieval Latin culture, from the outer reaches of Europe which, for the most part, were never colonised by Rome.

In these Gospel Books each of the four Gospels is prefaced by three illustrated pages, comprising an Evangelist portrait, a decorated cross and an ornate initial page. The decorated

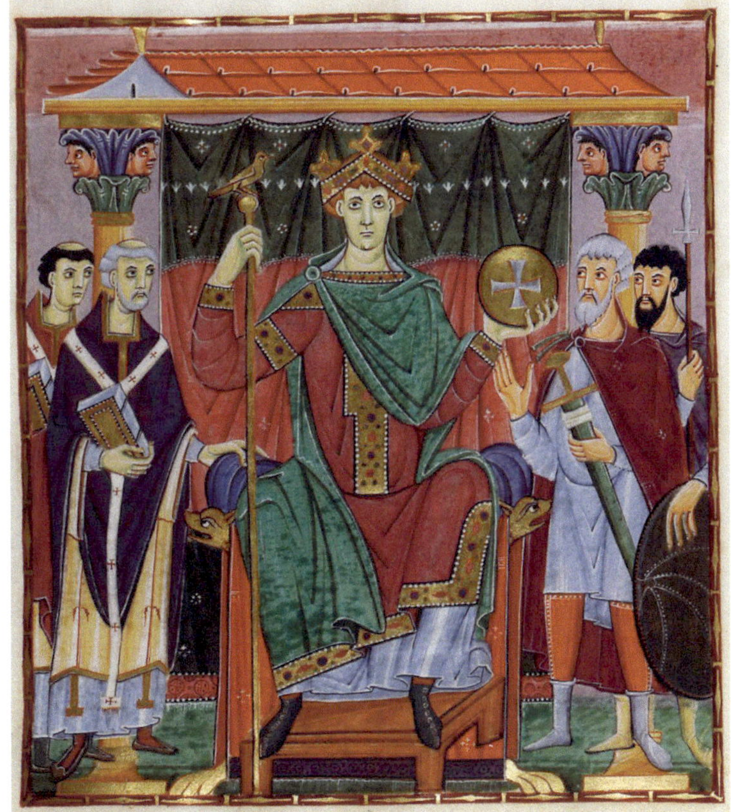

This portrait from a Gospel Book of *c*.998 shows the eighteen-year-old Holy Roman Emperor Otto III, the most powerful man in Western Europe. He is portrayed as an almost God-like figure, a reminder that religious manuscripts could also make political statements.

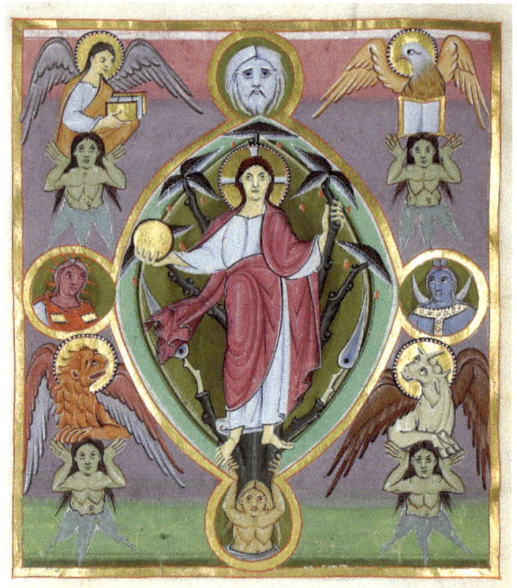

Christ in Majesty is flanked by the four Evangelists, seen here in a Gospel Book created for Heinrich, Holy Roman Emperor. Similar images regularly appeared before the Gospels.

Canon Tables, like this example from a Carolingian Gospel Book, cross-reference events in the life of Christ between the four Gospels, and are characteristically set in an architectural frame.

crosses are especially intricate in their decorative schemes, for which reason they are also known as carpet pages. The Book of Kells is the latest and most elaborate of the principal surviving Gospel Books produced by Irish monks, and includes what is thought to be the earliest pictorial representation of the Virgin and Child.

A fresh cultural impetus came with the rise in mainland Europe of Charlemagne, crowned Holy Roman Emperor by the Pope in 800. His court was in the modern German town of Aachen (or Aix-la-Chapelle). This Carolingian artistic renewal was influenced by the Insular style, which had spread to mainland Europe with monasteries of Irish foundation, including Bobbio (Italy), Luxeuil (France) and St Gall (Switzerland). Charlemagne brought in scribes and illuminators from far and wide, including the Mediterranean and Byzantium, as well as scholars, including Alcuin of York, who ran his cathedral schools. The Bibles and Gospel Books

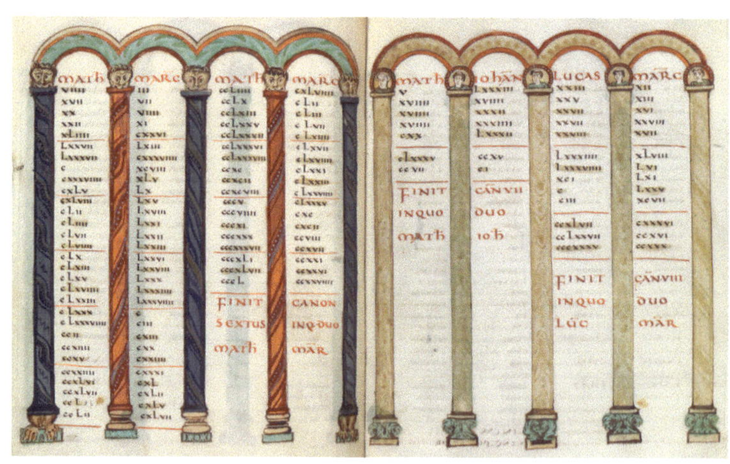

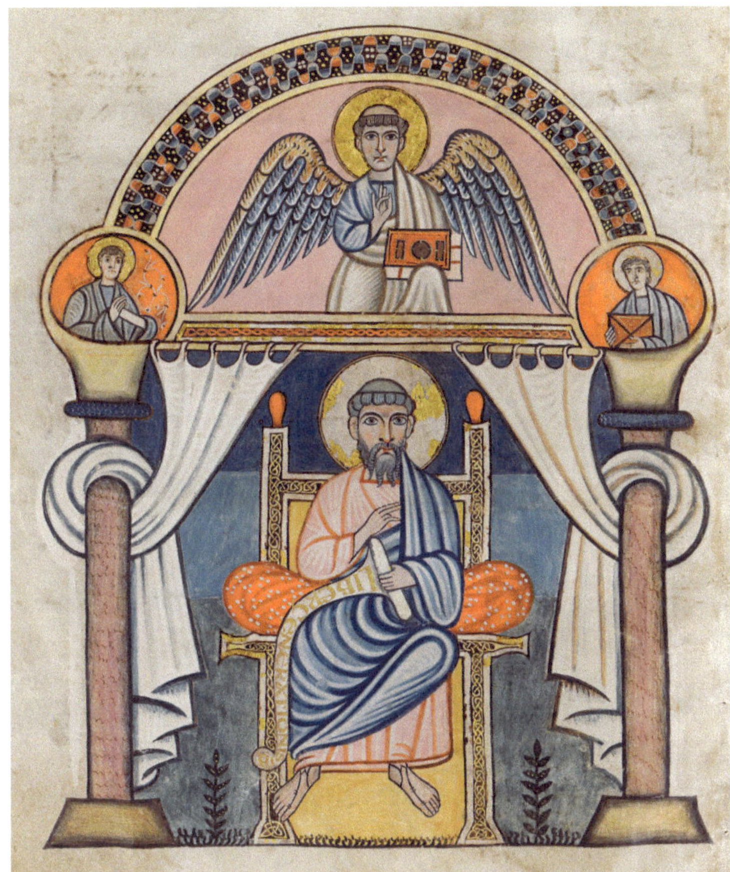

This miniature of St Matthew is from the eighth-century Codex Aureus made in Canterbury. He sits within a classical round arch, in the semi-circular tympanum of which is his Evangelist symbol, a winged angel holding a book.

produced for successive Holy Roman Emperors, some of which included portraits of the emperors themselves, are some of the most opulent books ever produced, intended to rival the richest treasures of eastern Christendom.

Insular and Carolingian Bibles followed a similar pattern of illustration. The prefatory material is illustrated with Canon Tables. Events in the life of Jesus appear in different places in each of the Gospels, so a table of concordance was devised in the fourth century by Eusebius of Caesarea by which means events in the life of Christ could be cross-referenced. These Canon Tables are always set in an architectural frame of

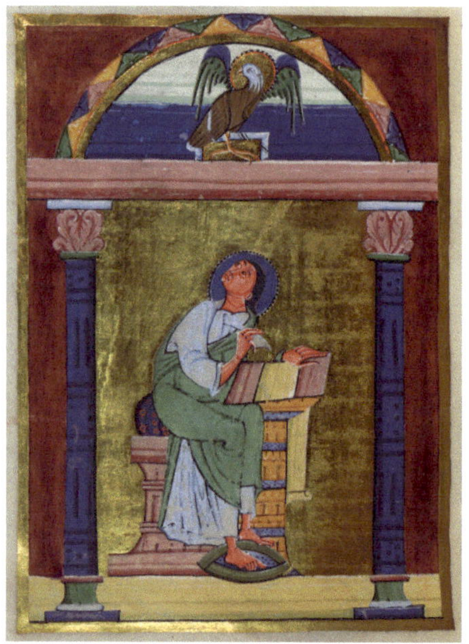

In this portrait of St John the Evangelist from an eleventh-century German Bible his symbol, the eagle, is in the tympanum of the arch.

columns and round arches, in a Roman classical style. Each of the Gospels was prefaced by a miniature of the Evangelists. They were always depicted holding or writing books, and with their symbols – an angel for Matthew, a lion for Mark, an ox for Luke and an eagle for John – framed by columns and round arches. Architectural frames placed the Gospel authors in a contemporary world, emphasising that the words of the Bible were not history but in the here and now.

Bible production had to keep pace with the foundation of new religious communities in the great age of monasticism. The range of illustrative material increased as artists could portray scenes to introduce the books of the Old and New Testaments, either as miniatures or historiated initials. Every religious community needed Bibles, both for private study and for reading aloud in church. A twelfth-century catalogue of books in Reading Abbey records four Bibles, three of which were in two volumes and one in three volumes. One of Reading's Bibles was left in the cloister for the monks to read, and in the fourteenth century one of the volumes was kept in the dormitory and was used for reading out loud at mealtimes in the refectory. These and other contemporary Bibles were extremely large, up to 20 by 14 inches, which meant that they were the fruit of monumental efforts and were intended to be placed on a lectern.

Division of the Bible into separate volumes, covering for example the Gospels and Psalms, encouraged the notion that scripture was a collection of separate texts which could be read in any order. In Paris in the early thirteenth century scribes began producing single-volume Bibles on thin vellum, with pages small enough to be easily portable. The order and names of the books of the Bible were standardised and the texts were divided up into numbered chapters, a scheme which has survived to this day (chapters acquired verse numbers only in the sixteenth century). This is usually ascribed to the influence of Stephen Langton (*c*.1150–1228), who taught in Paris before he was elected Archbishop of Canterbury in 1207.

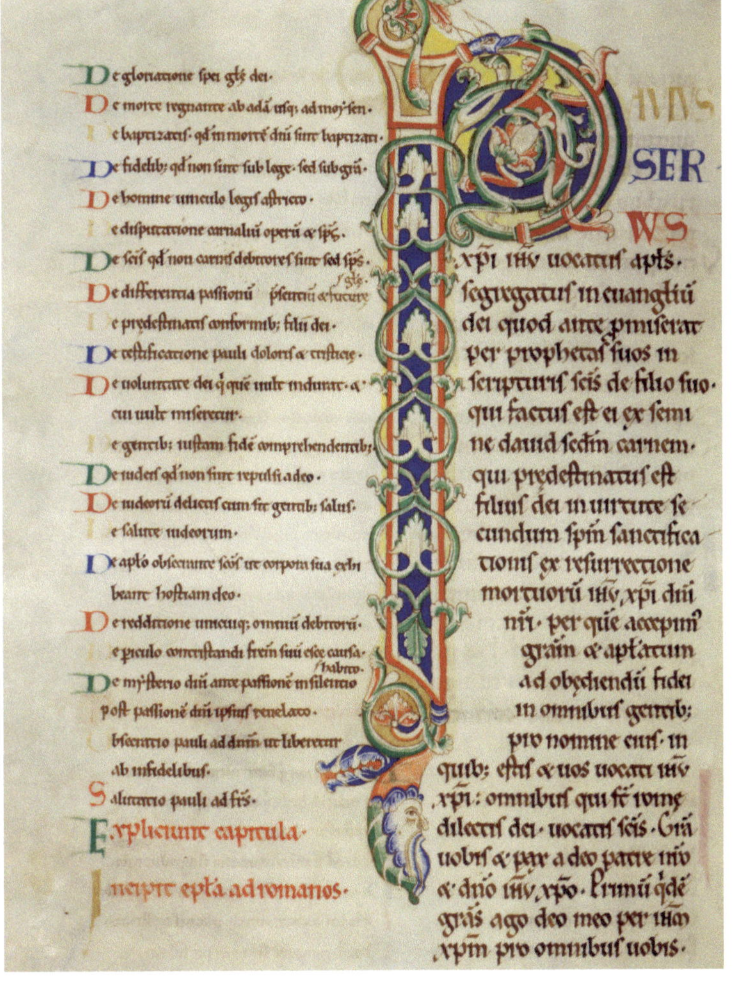

The opening of St Paul's Epistle to the Romans is written in a pre-Gothic script in this large-format New Testament produced *c*.1130 and used at Rochester Cathedral Priory. The intertwined foliage of the initial terminates at the base in a foliate head. Compare this with the image on page 15, which shows the same page in minuscule script.

In this thirteenth-century English pocket Bible God speaks to the prophet in an historiated initial at the beginning of the Book of Jeremiah.

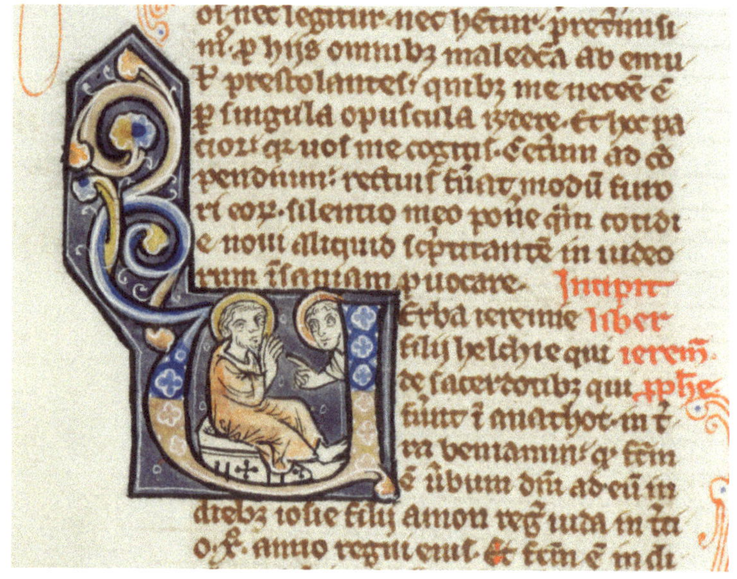

The new Dominican order of Friars, with a strong presence in Paris, was instrumental in the production and dissemination of one-volume Bibles. The Bible was essential to Dominican teaching and its friars went out into the world as preachers, by which means the books were imported into England. Production of Bibles was prolific in the mid-thirteenth century and, given the longevity of books in the Middle Ages, filled the western world with most of the Bibles it needed until the invention of the printing press.

BOOKS FOR RITUAL

Christian observance is defined by ritual, including the daily rituals of the Mass, seasonal rituals around Easter and saints' feast days, and one-off rituals of baptism and funeral. There had always been Bibles and psalm books in church, but as rituals were refined and standardised, books for ritual use started to be produced in the twelfth century. Eventually they became compulsory for all churches. But these books were for the use of the priests rather than the congregation. Apart from the fact that there was no universal literacy in medieval Britain, the texts were in Latin rather than English or Welsh. Nevertheless, parishioners could and often did commission and donate them to the parish as an act of piety. Most are purely functional, but the more prestigious are among the most richly illuminated of manuscripts.

The most important service books were the Breviary and the Missal. The Breviary was the book of the divine office for monks and others in holy orders, which divided the day into eight canonical hours. This was a daily round of prayers and anthems chanted in the choir of the church. The first two offices, Matins and Lauds, were sung before dawn. The others were Prime, Terce, Sext, Nones, Vespers and Compline. They included hymns, Bible readings, psalms and prayers. Monks used them daily, but parishes often owned their own copies for the priest to recite Matins and Vespers. Although it was not necessary to provide illuminations in a book from which it was intended to recite, some breviaries are richer than others according to the status of their users. One of the best known is the Chichele Breviary, commissioned by Henry Chichele,

BELOW LEFT
Clerics sing from a choir book in the inhabited initial 'C', from a fourteenth-century French Breviary.

BELOW RIGHT
Most illuminated Missals include a full-page image of the Crucifixion, which marks the beginning of the canon of the Mass, the prayers said by the priest as bread and wine are ritually transformed into the body and blood of Christ.

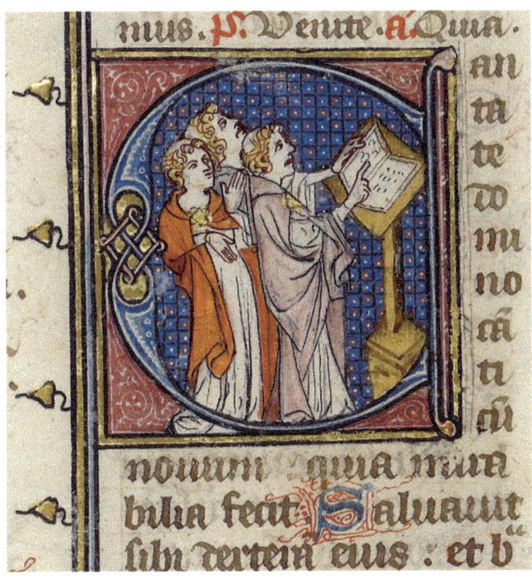

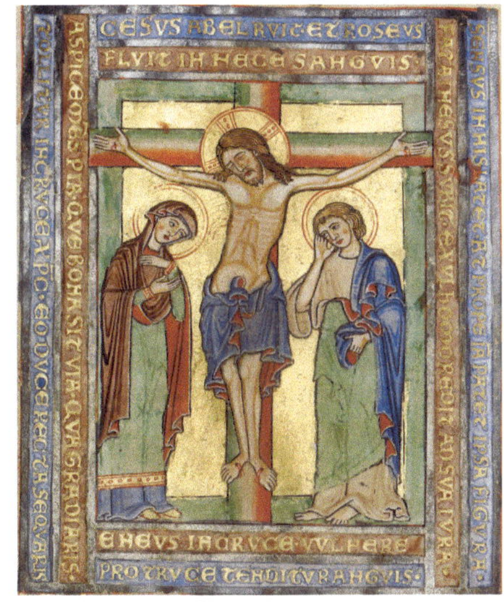

erstwhile bishop of St David's who was elected Archbishop of Canterbury in 1414. The fashion for illuminated breviaries came late in the Middle Ages, and many were commissioned by wealthy patrons. Margaret of York (1446–1503), the Duchess of Burgundy and sister to Edward IV and Richard III, was a dedicated manuscript collector and commissioned a lavish Breviary for herself from Ghent in the 1470s.

The Missal was a different kind of book. It was the book of the Mass and could be used only by a priest at the altar. The core of the book was the unchanging liturgy of the Eucharist, but it also contained the different hymns, prayers and readings specified for the time of year, as well as requiem masses, an important part of medieval Christian worship. Missals were not normally elaborately illustrated but they could contain devotional images of the Crucifixion and Christ in Glory (an image of the enthroned Christ as ruler of the world). In a Missal the miniatures cannot really be said to merely illustrate the

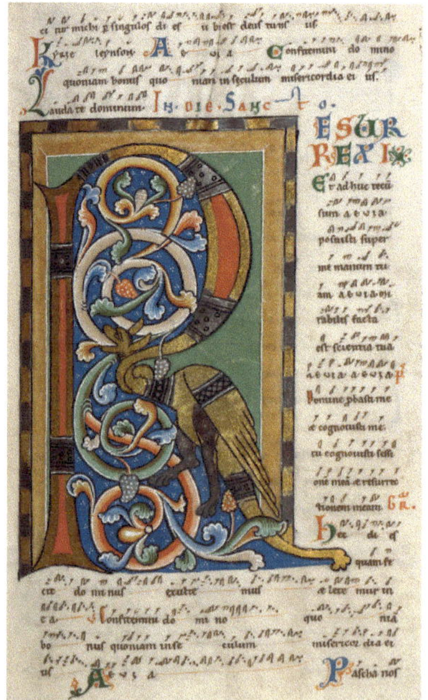

This decorated initial 'R' begins the Mass for Easter in a rare, richly decorated Missal from the late twelfth century, produced in Germany.

text. During the Mass the bread and wine of the Eucharist are transformed into the body and blood of Christ, and this mystical element applies to the miniatures in the Missal. Like icons, they became the things that they represent, and were another affirmation of the presence of God in the sanctuary of the church.

Missals were among the service books that were destroyed in England and Wales at the time of the Reformation,

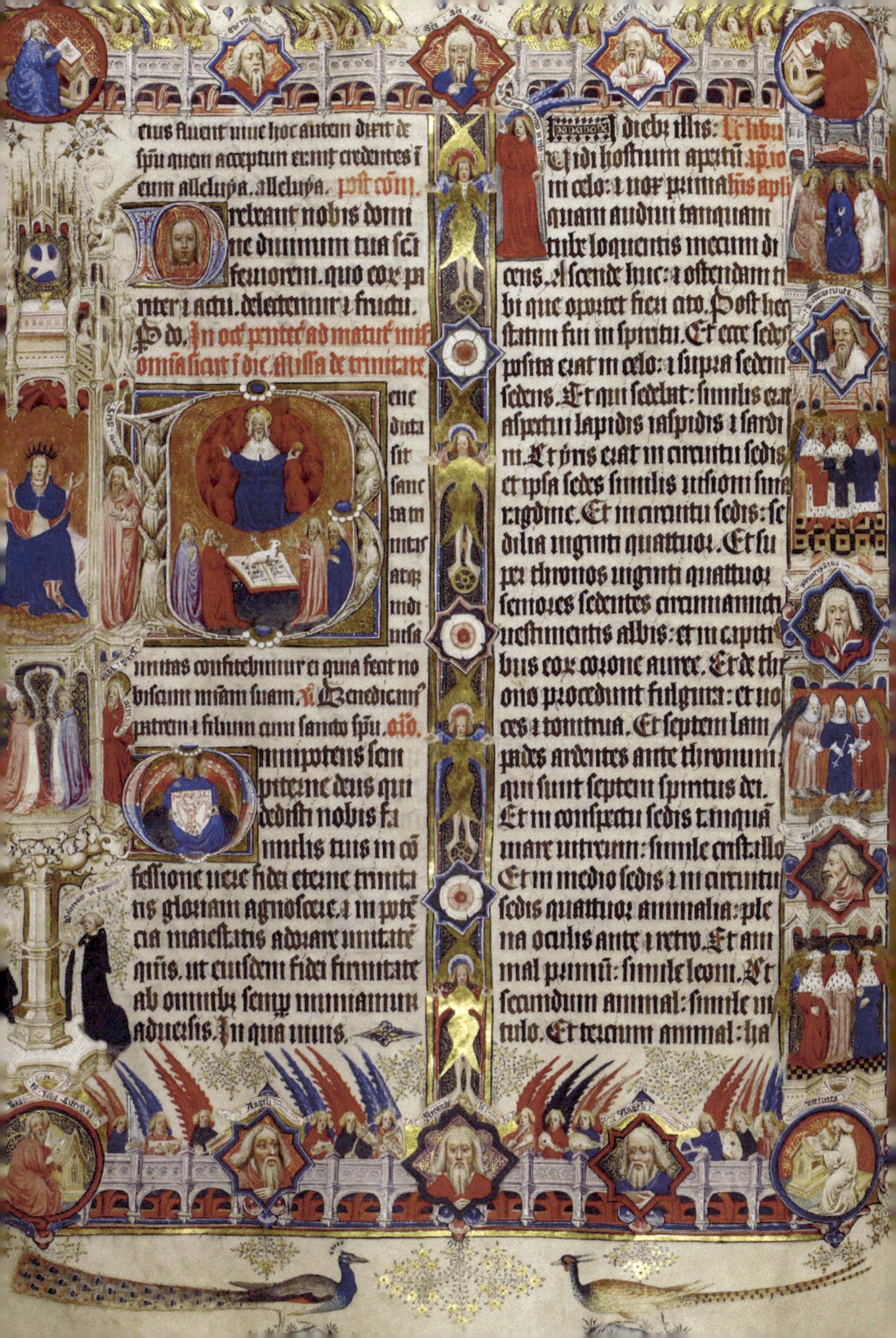

eius sumit vine hoc autem dixit de
spiritu quem accepturi erant credentes in
eum alleluya. alleluya. post com.
Proficiant nobis domine
ne dona tua scilicet
senioribus. quo cor pa-
riter et actu. deleentur et fructu.
Sequitur. In die penthec. ad matutinas missa
omnia sicut in die. Missa de trinitate.

B
...ene
dicta
sit
sanc
ta in
nitas
atque
indi
uisa
vinitas confitebimur ei quia fecit no-
biscum misericordiam suam. R. Benedicamus
patrem et filium cum sancto spiritu. oratio.

Omnipotens sem-
piterne deus qui
dedisti nobis fa-
mulis tuis in con-
fessione vere fidei eterne trinitatis gloriam agnoscere. et in poten-
cia maiestatis adorare unitatem
trinitatis. ut eiusdem fidei firmitate
ab omnibus semper muniamur
aduersis. In qua uiuis.

In diebus illis: Et vidi
hostium apertum ipso
in celo: et vox prima alis apli
quam audivi tanquam
tube loquentis mecum di-
cens. Ascende huc: et ostendam ti-
bi que oportet fieri cito. Post hec
statim fui in spiritu. Et ecce sedes
posita erat in celo: et supra sedem
sedens. Et qui sedebat: similis erat
aspectui lapidis iaspidis et sardi-
nis. Et yris erat in circuitu sedis:
et ipsa sedes similis visioni sma-
ragdine. Et in circuitu sedis: se-
dilia uiginti quattuor. Et super thronos uiginti quattuor
seniores sedentes circumamicti
uestimentis albis: et in capiti-
bus eorum corone auree. Et de thr-
ono procedunt fulgura: et uo-
ces et tonitrua. Et septem lam-
pades ardentes ante thronum:
qui sunt septem spiritus dei.
Et in conspectu sedis: tanquam
mare uitreum: simile cristallo.
Et in medio sedis et in circuitu
sedis quattuor: animalia: ple-
na oculis ante et retro. Et animal primum: simile leoni. Et
secundum animal: simile ui-
tulo. Et tercium animal: ha-

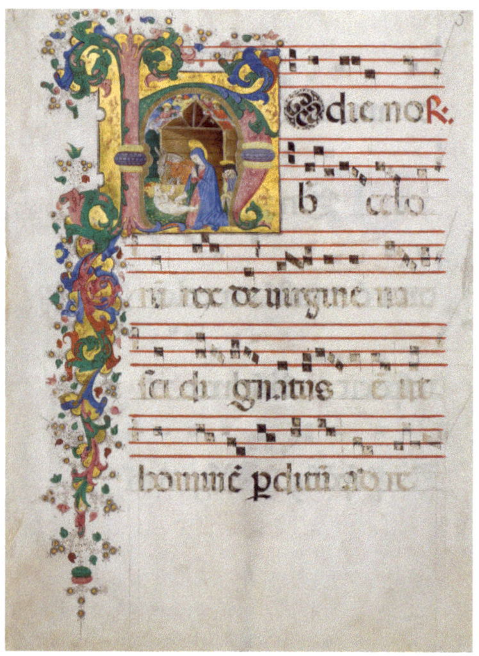

The Nativity is depicted in an historiated initial 'h' from a fifteenth-century Antiphoner.

when the Mass was abolished in favour of the Protestant Eucharist. Few of them were valuable works of art and many were written by the parish priests themselves. On a different scale are the expensive books donated by wealthy donors as an act of piety. Their portraits, or coats of arms, can be found in the margins of the miniatures of the Crucifixion. The most lavish Missals were commissioned by bishops, often for their own use. The Sherborne Missal is one of the most luxurious English Missals to have survived. It was commissioned by the abbot of Sherborne at the beginning of the fifteenth century, and executed by the scribe John Whas and illuminator John Siferwas.

Worship was accompanied by musical chants which were traditionally said to date from the time of Gregory the Great (died 604). The two principal forms of music books were the Gradual for use in the Mass, and the Antiphoner for use with the divine offices. Marks above lines of text denoted musical notes in choir books from at least the tenth century, but the music was expressed more clearly after the invention of the stave in the thirteenth century. Decoration of music books depended upon the wealth and status of the donor, just as it did with other service books.

BOOKS FOR PRAYER AND CONTEMPLATION

Until 1200, books were produced primarily for use by priests, but lay piety flourished from the thirteenth century and the market for illuminated manuscripts therefore expanded.

Reading was an act of devotion, while prayer was at the core of Christian worship. All Christians knew that they faced Judgement, and that, before they could enter heaven, they would have to undergo a period of purgatory during which their sins were cleansed. The period of purgatory which a person could expect to endure was reduced according to the good works that had been performed on Earth. These good works included Christian observance and commissioning beautiful books, whether for personal use or for donation to a church. Prayers for the dead were central to religious observance, done in the knowledge that the living would one day need the prayers of subsequent generations. Investment in a book that contained readings and prayers, and which was also a valuable work of art, was therefore economically expensive but spiritually wise.

Psalters were originally liturgical books owned by monasteries and other churches, but later they were bought by wealthy lay people and became the vehicle for some of the richest illuminations in the Middle Ages. A Psalter is a book of psalms, one of the most important books of the Old Testament, comprising 150 ancient songs grouped together, and traditionally said to have been composed by King David. Apart from the psalms themselves a Psalter might contain Biblical songs of praise, known as canticles, drawn from other Old Testament books, intercessory prayers to saints, and a calendar. It was also the ancestor of books of the divine office, including the Breviary and

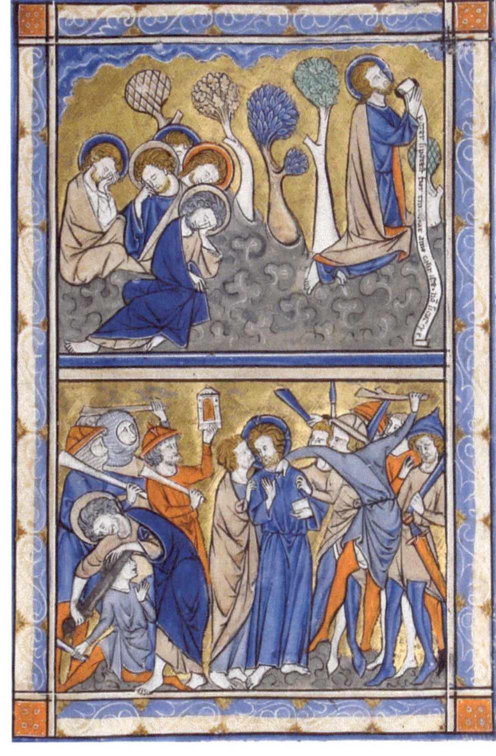

This miniature shows two scenes from the Passion – Christ praying in the Garden of Gethsemane and his subsequent betrayal by Judas Iscariot – and appeared in a Psalter made in England c.1270, probably for Eleanor of Provence, Henry III's queen.

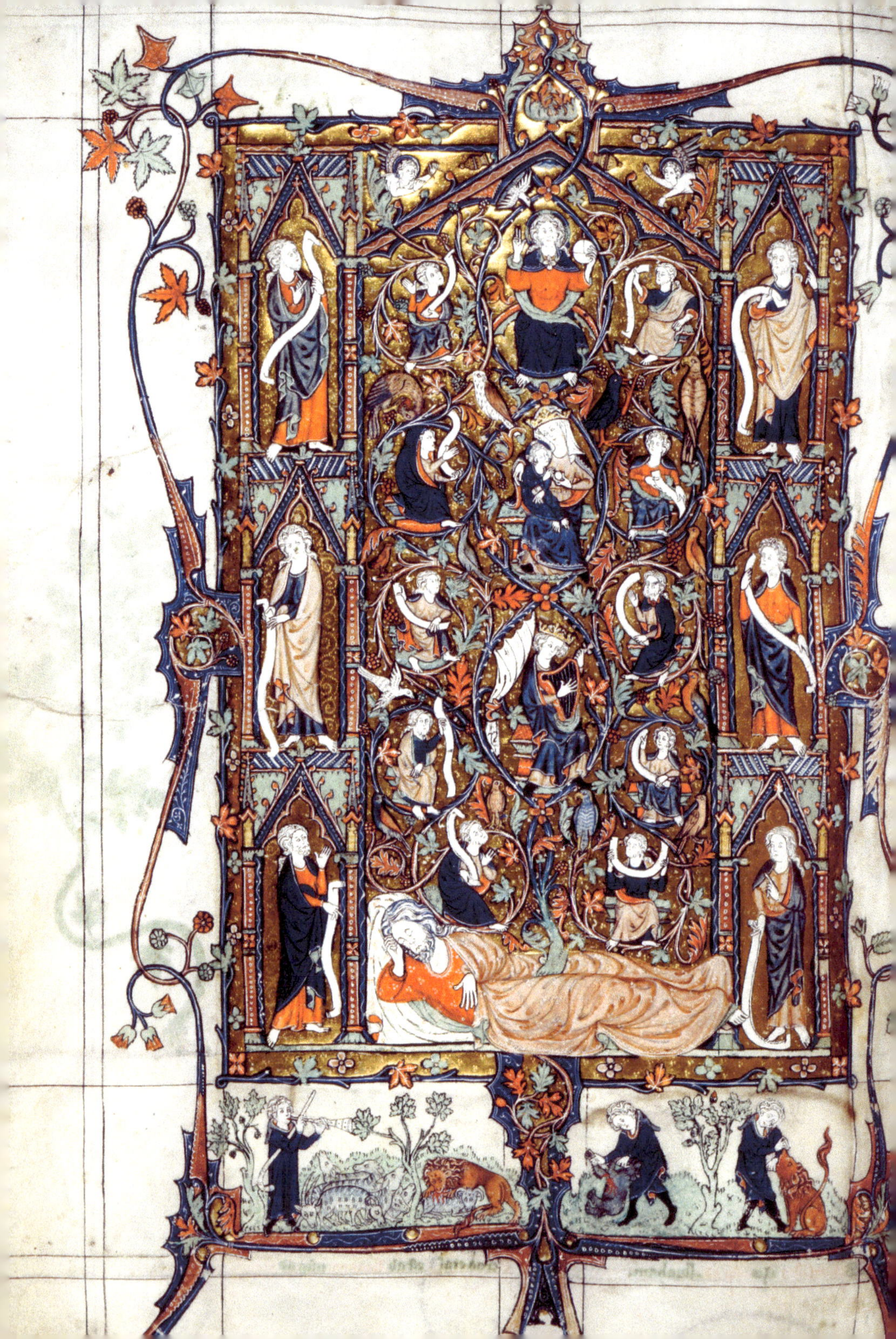

Book of Hours. Recitation of the psalms depended upon the liturgical calendar and so, although in many cases the psalms were presented in their Biblical order, sometimes they were organised according to liturgical order, which is known as a ferial Psalter. The importance of the liturgical year was the reason that Psalters contained calendars.

Psalters were among the earliest of Christian books. The Vespasian Psalter, now in the British Library, was produced at the abbey of St Augustine in Canterbury *c.*730. Even though the traditionally held belief that it was written by Augustine himself and brought with him on his mission in 597 turned out to be false, the book nevertheless remained in possession of the abbey for 800 years. It is one of the earliest luxuriously illustrated Psalters and is one of the earliest books to incorporate historiated initials. Psalters were often more richly illuminated than Bibles largely because so many were owned by individuals rather than institutions. A good example is the St Albans Psalter commissioned by Geoffrey de Gorham, abbot of St Albans between 1119 and 1146, which was possibly intended initially for use at the monastery, but was presented to Christina of Markyate, an anchoress who lived under the protection of the abbot. It is a richly decorated piece of work, with initials used at the beginning of each psalm. There are forty miniatures depicting the life of Christ and a calendar giving church feast days and illustrated with the Labours of the Months.

OPPOSITE
The Tree of Jesse is a pictorial representation of the genealogy of Christ, in the form of a tree with Jesse, father of David, at its root. The subject was popular in Psalters, as in this English example of *c.*1310.

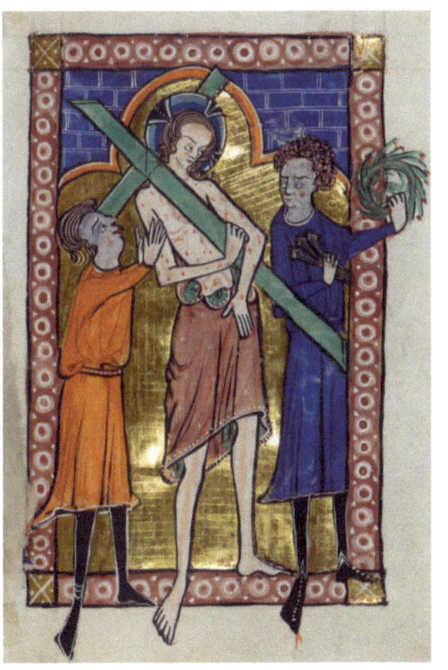

Christ carrying the cross is part of a prefatory cycle of illuminations depicting the life, death and resurrection of Christ in the thirteenth-century Carrow Psalter, made in East Anglia.

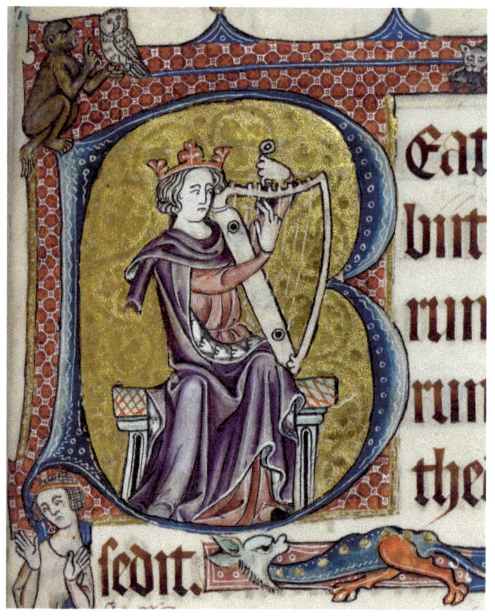

David was often portrayed playing the harp in Psalters. This example from the fourteenth-century Luttrell Psalter also shows an ape confiding with an owl (upper left).

Once it had acquired a lay as well as a religious readership, the Psalter was the book with which many people learned to read. Most Psalters for church use are relatively plain, and were well used and so have survived poorly. Psalters for private lay use saw much less practical use and were often profusely illustrated. The Psalter commissioned by Sir Geoffrey Luttrell in the second quarter of the fourteenth century is especially richly illustrated, with marginal scenes including contemporary rural life (Luttrell had a large estate) and grotesques, imagined hybrid creatures that can be in turn hideous or just humorous. The book was produced in Lincolnshire and is the work of a single scribe and five artists.

Decorated initials were important in helping the reader navigate the psalms. The most important was the Beatus initial, based on the 'B' of *Beatus vir*, 'blessed is the man', which is the opening of Psalm 1. Psalms were illustrated with scenes from the life of David, as well as depicting events and characters from the psalms themselves. Later Psalters are more likely to have a prefatory cycle of miniatures illustrating Christ's Passion (the events leading up to his crucifixion) or Old Testament stories, and perhaps also miniatures of saints if the book contained intercessory prayers.

After Psalters, the other portion of the Bible that achieved popularity with both religious and lay readers was the Apocalypse, an illustrated Book of Revelation, usually with commentaries on the text. An alternative title was a *Beatus*, named after the eighth-century monk St Beatus from Liébana

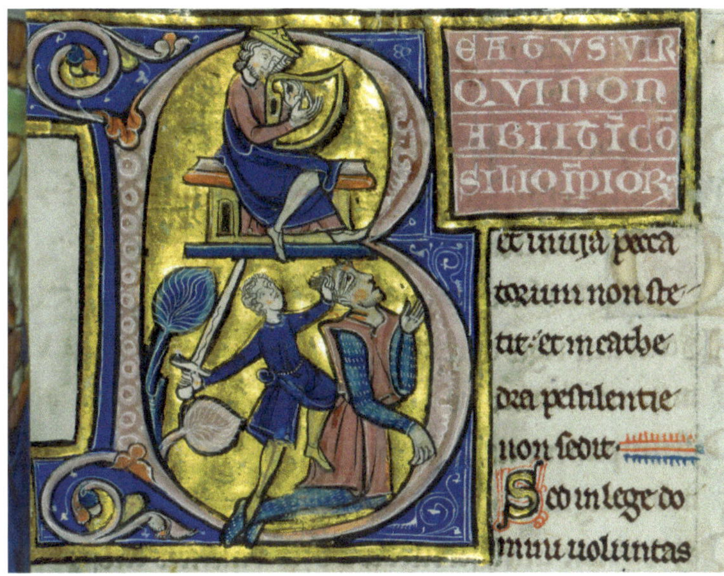

This historiated initial 'B' (for *Beatus vir*, or 'blessed is the man') at the beginning of Psalm 1 depicts David playing the harp and slaying Goliath. It appears in a Flemish Psalter of *c.*1265–80.

in northern Spain whose commentary was incorporated into the book. Beatus manuscripts were especially popular in Spain in the tenth and eleventh centuries. The Book of Revelation, as it is known in the Protestant tradition, deals with the visions of St John the Divine, and introduced such familiar concepts as New Jerusalem, the Antichrist and the Last Judgement.

This historiated initial from a fourteenth-century East Anglian Psalter shows three men waist-deep in water. It is the opening of Psalm 69, which begins 'Save me, O God, for the waters have come up to my neck'.

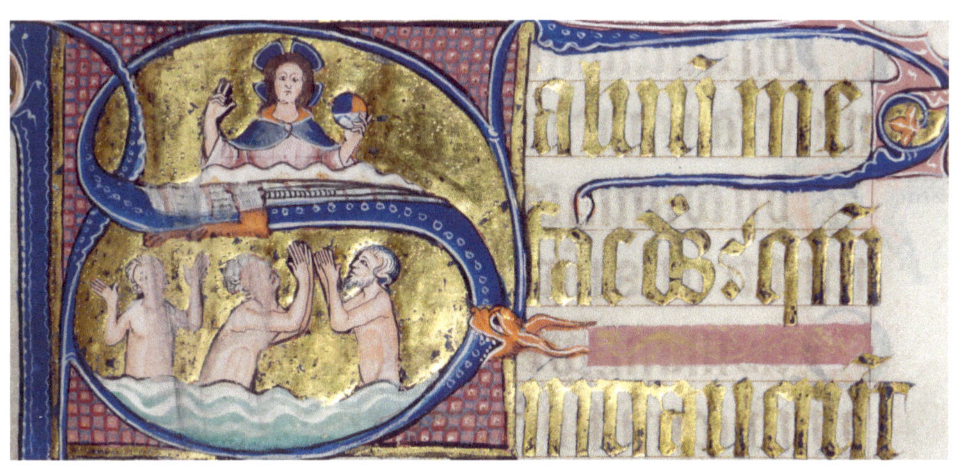

Medieval Christians confidently expected the world to end. Early theologians assumed that the universe was divided into six equal ages, based on an interpretation of the six days of creation, and that they were living in the last of them. In the Bible St Peter equates one day in the eyes of God with a thousand years on Earth. It was logical, therefore, to assume that the world would end in the year AD 1000, or failing that, in the year 1033 to account for the time of Christ's crucifixion rather than his birth. That is why Apocalypse manuscripts were prevalent in the tenth century, but they became so again, especially in England, in the thirteenth century, in consequence of a different interpretation of scripture. Revelation described the 'woman clothed with the sun' who gave birth to a son and then escaped to the wilderness for 1,260 days. On the basis of a day for a year in the eyes of God, there was renewed interest in Apocalypse manuscripts timed to the end of the world in 1260, or 1293.

St John's visions concerned the struggles between good and evil leading up to the Last Judgement, when the kingdom of heaven, or New Jerusalem, will be established for the chosen few, and sinners will be condemned to eternal damnation. Illustrations helped with the interpretations of the text. St John sometimes features in all of these, receiving his visions from an angel, being shown New Jerusalem, and seeing the horsemen of the Apocalypse. Each of St John's visions provided an opportunity for the artist, partly because the writing is dramatic and visual. Successive clarion calls of the angels heralded hail and fire, a burning mountain

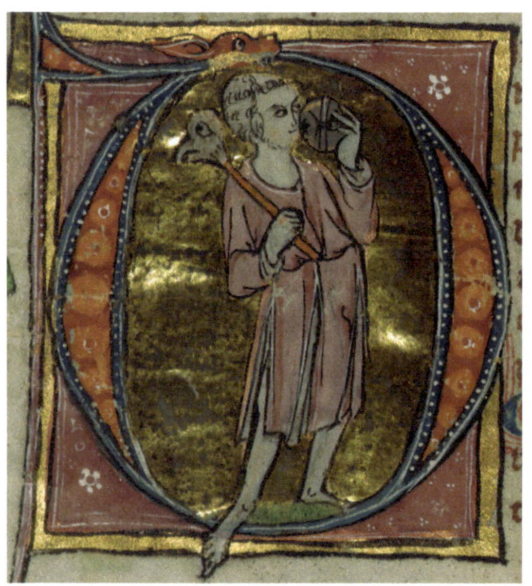

This historiated initial illustrates Psalm 53, in which God talks of evildoers 'who devour my people as men eat bread', from an early fourteenth-century Flemish Psalter.

thrown into the sea, the sun, moon and stars darkening, an eagle crying woe to the inhabitants of the Earth, and a plague of locusts torturing the people without the seal of God in their foreheads. For a readership that believed in the end of the world and the Last Judgement these were powerful images, leaving the reader in no doubt that time was running out to expiate their own sins. Hell is shown as a world of monstrous beasts, gaping hell mouths, torment by fire, nature turned on its head as birds eat human flesh. All this is contrasted with scenes of the chosen dressed in their white robes and holding palm branches. The vivid and

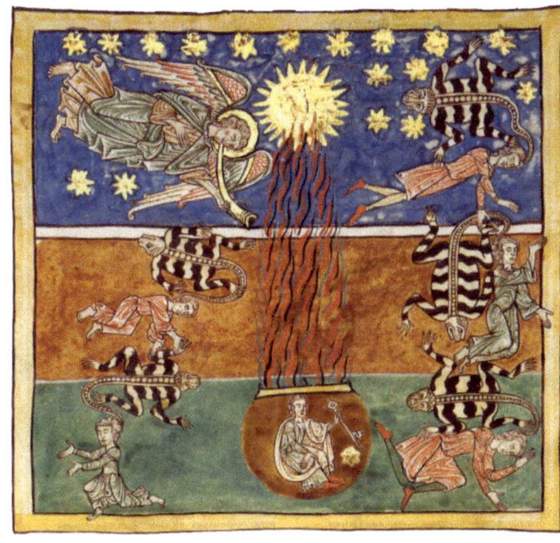

A Spanish *Beatus* manuscript of *c.*1180 illustrates the Clarion of the Fifth Angel's Trumpet from the Book of Revelation. A star fell from the sky and opened an abyss, from which smoke rose from a furnace, bringing with it a swarm of locusts.

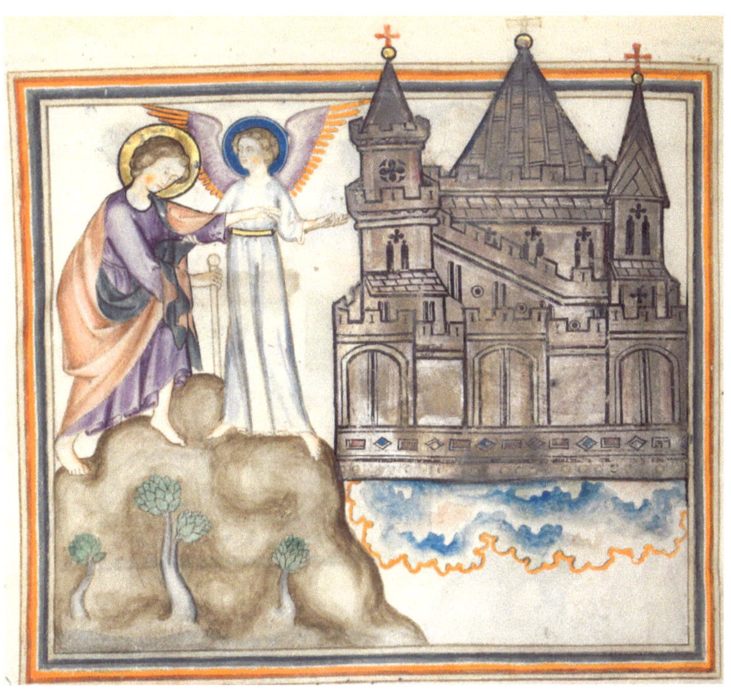

St John the Divine is led to New Jerusalem, from the The Cloisters Apocalypse, produced in northern France *c.*1330.

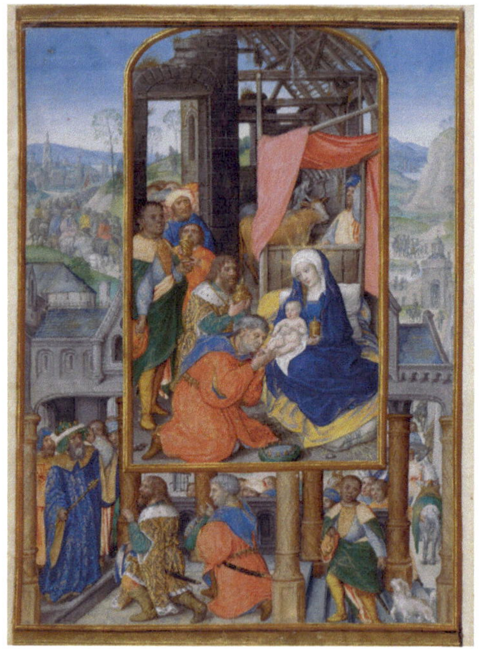

This miniature of the Adoration of the Magi is from a Book of Hours of the early sixteenth century and was illustrated by Gerard Horenbout of Ghent, who created works for royalty including James IV of Scotland.

dramatic imagery belonged to the devil's side and the artists seem to have relished most the visions of humanity's comeuppance.

The Psalter for church use evolved into a book of more practical benefit for lay people known as a Book of Hours. Books of Hours (known as *Horae* in Latin) are the most commonly surviving medieval illuminated manuscripts, and the most profusely illustrated. This kind of book developed for lay people who wanted to introduce a more structured religious devotion. Ritual in the medieval church was male-dominated, with little direct input from lay people. The Mass was performed by the parish priest on behalf of the congregation, who were essentially spectators, while the divine offices were sung in cloistered detachment from everyday life. The Book of Hours included an abbreviated form of the divine office found in the Breviary, and gave lay people the opportunity to partake more profoundly in ritual observance than they had hitherto been able.

Books of Hours appeared first in the thirteenth century in France, Flanders and England, usually small enough to be carried in a pocket. Aristocrats and royalty were the first to commission them and their popularity then filtered down to other social classes. Some were status or political symbols. In 1423 John of Lancaster, the first Duke of Bedford, gave as a wedding present to his wife a lavish Book of Hours produced in Paris. Seven years later she in turn presented the book as a Christmas gift to the nine-year-old king of England, her nephew Henry VI. Margaret Tudor, daughter of Henry VII, and her husband James IV of Scotland, had a Book of Hours made for them at around the time of their marriage in 1503. The book, made in Ghent or Bruges, shows Mary kneeling as she recites the Hours of the Virgin.

Books of Hours were produced on a large scale for readers, most of whom had never before owned a book. In the fourteenth century Paris emerged as the leading source of manufacture. Booksellers by the Seine took orders and commissioned artists to produce them, often, it seems, hiring more than one artist for different sections of a book. In the fifteenth century Books of Hours were produced across France, as well as in England, Italy and Flanders (they were less popular in Germany). Many of the books sold to English owners were produced in Paris, Ghent or Bruges.

A Book of Hours usually opened with a calendar, similar to the ones that were included in Psalters. Although many Books of Hours used in England were produced abroad, scribes would tailor their calendars to include popular English and local saints. Each month is usually illustrated with a scene from everyday life and a zodiac sign. Calendar scenes offer an insight into the contemporary

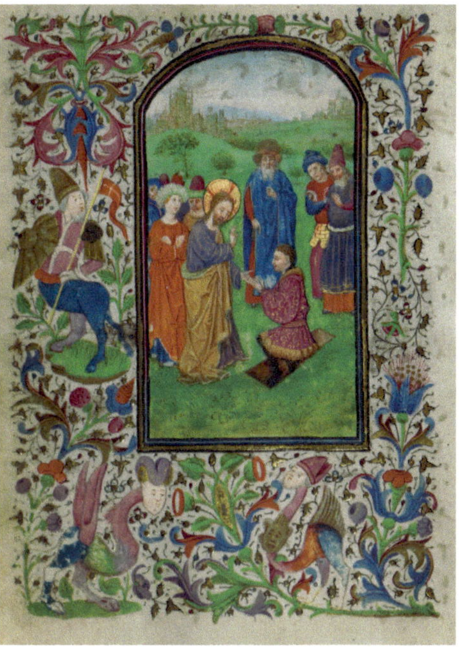

In this fifteenth-century Flemish Book of Hours different artists worked on the miniatures and the borders. The Raising of Lazarus illustrates Monday in the offices for the days of the week.

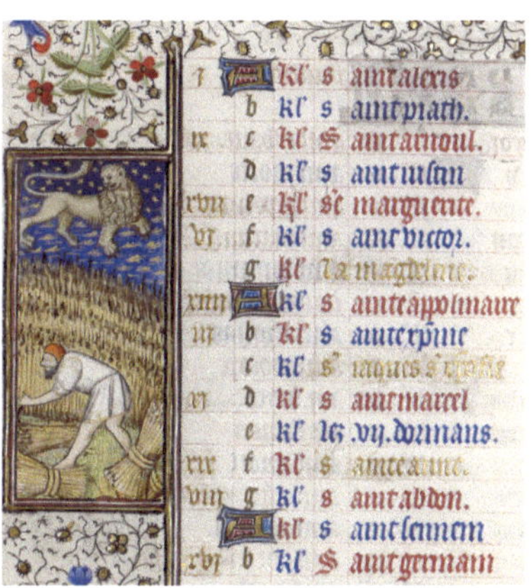

In a detail from a fifteenth-century calendar a man reaps in August under the sign of Leo.

medieval world and are generally restricted to rural life, even though many of the illustrations were made by artists in cities. Calendars may offer snapshots of rural life in the Middle Ages, but they were rarely drawn from nature. Scenes such as ploughing in February, sowing in March, harvesting in July, and knocking down acorns to fatten pigs in November were standard in calendars and were simply copied from other calendars.

The core of the Book of Hours is the Hours of the Virgin, the series of prayers and psalms recited in honour of the Virgin Mary at each of the canonical hours. Some books had other devotional sequences as well, such as the Hours of the Immaculate Conception, Hours of the Cross and Hours of the Holy Spirit. This emphasis on the Virgin Mary is thought to be one reason why Books of Hours were especially popular with women. The owner of the book was meant to pause eight times a day and to recite the hours in private, but we do not know how often these rigours were followed. The fifteenth-century theologian Jean Quentin, acknowledging that the demands of the book would defeat most people, recommended at least that Matins and Lauds should be recited before leaving the bedchamber. Many surviving copies, including the most luxurious, are in a condition that suggests they were little used, and perhaps the plainer copies were more often used for daily prayer.

An illuminated Hours of the Virgin Mary provided a visual narrative for private contemplation

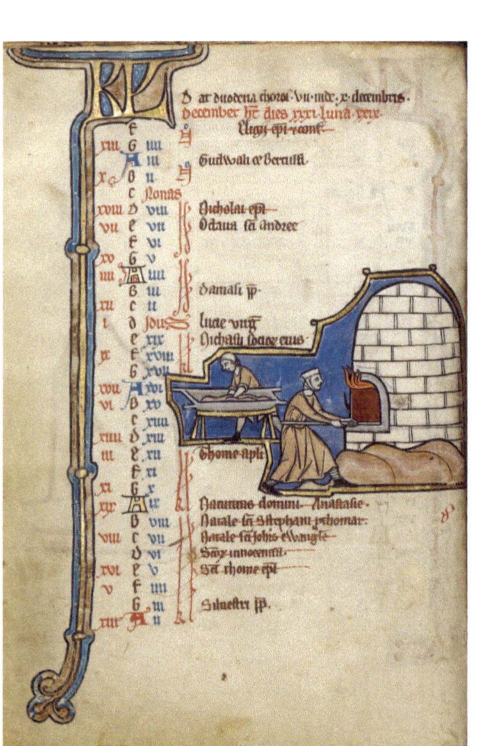

Baking is the chosen image for December in this mid-thirteenth-century Book of Hours made in Bruges.

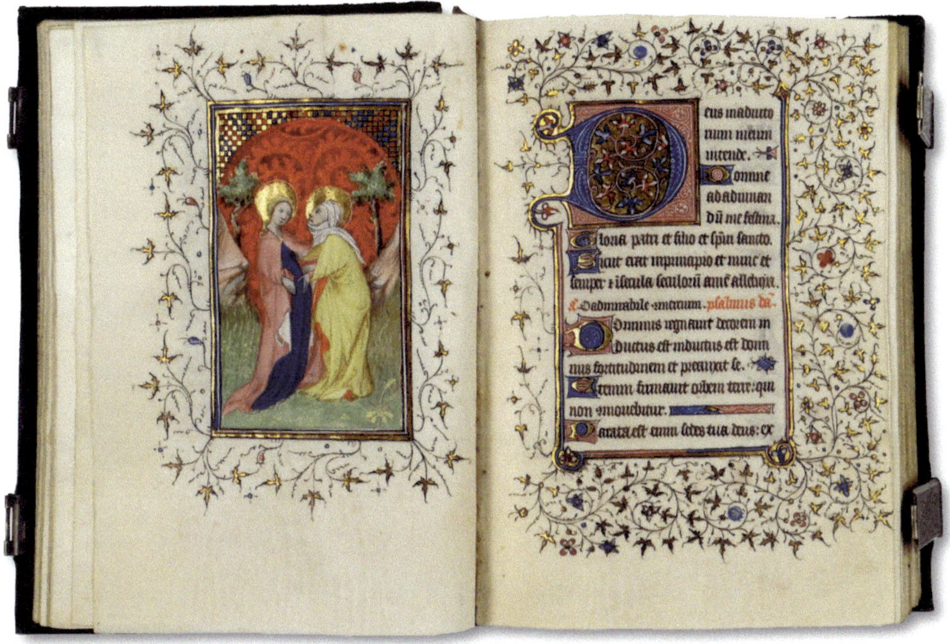

and reflection while reciting the words that glorified her in prayer. The images were familiar and reassuring, perhaps just as revered as the text. The number of illuminations varied according to the scheme of the book and the budget of the customer. The richest Books of Hours have an illumination at the beginning of each of the hours, conforming to the narrative of her life. The Annunciation, where the Archangel Gabriel tells Mary she is to have a child, appears at the beginning of Matins, while for Lauds the opening image is the Visitation, the scene in which Mary met Elizabeth, mother of John the Baptist. Other illuminations concern Mary and the life of the young Christ, beginning with the Nativity for Prime and including well-known events in the Bible such as the Adoration of the Magi for Sext and the Presentation in the Temple for Nones. The latter was the rite by which Jesus was named and circumcised, and Mary was ritually purified after childbirth (2 February or Candlemas in the

The meeting of Mary with Elizabeth, mother of John the Baptist, who greeted her with the words 'Blessed are you among women', was an important illustration accompanying the Hours of the Virgin, here in a Flemish Book of Hours made c.1420 for the English market.

The Adoration of the Magi precedes Sext in the Hours of the Virgin, shown here in a Flemish Book of Hours of the late fifteenth century.

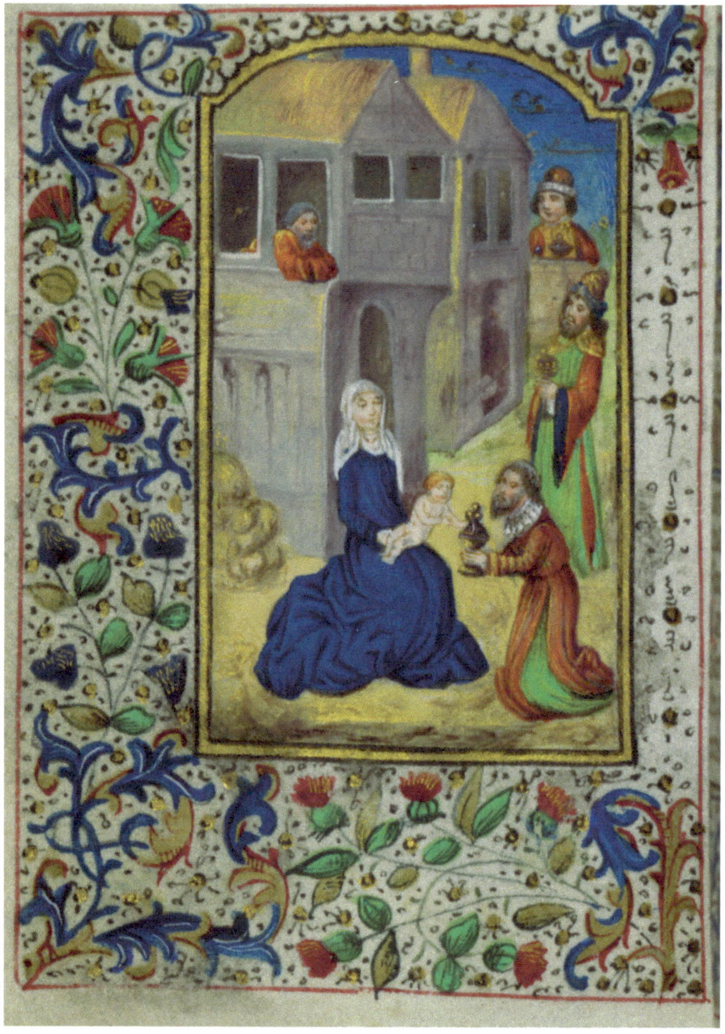

medieval Christian calendar). The sequence ended with the Flight into Egypt, accompanying Compline, when Joseph and Mary took the child Christ away from the massacre of infants ordered by King Herod.

Other 'Hours' would have their own visual narratives, and would include images such as the Pentecost (the descent of the Holy Spirit) for the Hours of the Holy Spirit, and scenes from

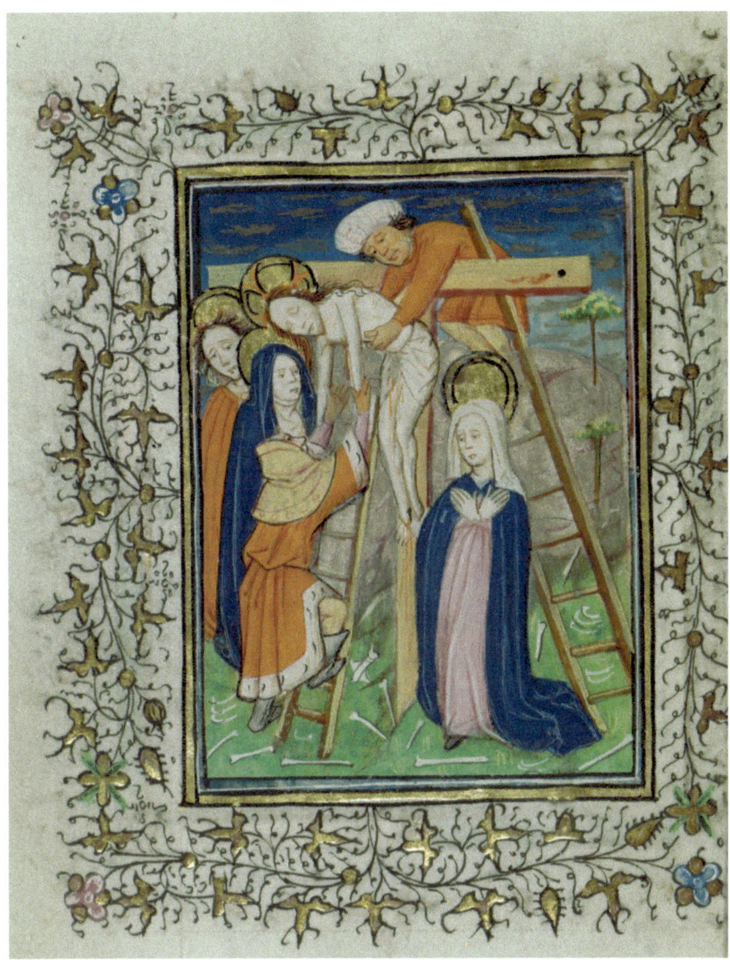

A miniature of the deposition from the cross precedes the office of Vespers in the Hours of the Cross, as shown in this fifteenth-century Flemish Book of Hours.

the Passion, including the Crucifixion, for the Hours of the Cross. The Hours are followed by seven penitential psalms, on the theme of forgiveness, and a litany of saints which asks forgiveness for sins. As medieval Christianity was much concerned with death and the need to seek forgiveness of sins before dying, prayers in the Book of Hours offered a safeguard against sudden death. Appropriate illustrations included the Last Judgement. Finally, there would be the office of the dead, comprising more psalms and readings collected in order to be said around the coffin, but recited on a daily basis as a reminder of mortality. This office was usually illustrated with no more than a single miniature, portraying one part of the medieval funeral service.

Special individual prayers, known as suffrages, were often added at the end of the Book, usually asking a saint to give protection from specific dangers, such as childbirth and sudden death. However, the choice of saints was very personal and it was common to have prayers, and a miniature, to a namesake of the book's owner. Individual saints did not need to be named because they could be identified according to their attributes, usually, but not always, associated with their martyrdom. St Margaret is shown as a dragon slayer and often appears in Books of Hours because she was patron saint of childbirth. St Christopher, patron saint of travellers and a popular medieval saint who was often depicted on the walls of parish churches, is shown carrying the child Christ across a stream. St James, patron saint of pilgrims with a cult centred on Compostella in Spain, holds a pilgrim staff. The popularity of some saints was geographically confined. The most prominent English saint of the Middle Ages was St Thomas Becket, the Archbishop of Canterbury who was murdered at the altar in 1170. The cult of St Edmund, by contrast, was largely confined to his former kingdom of East Anglia.

Since the Book of Hours was not a liturgical book, it had no fixed formula and numerous variations were made to suit the customer and his or her budget. There were also slight

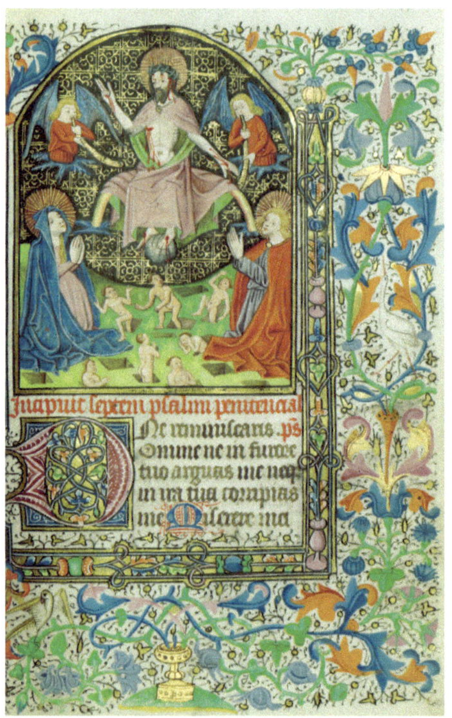

The Last Judgement precedes the seven penitential psalms in a Book of Hours.

variations in the verses and responses of the Hours, according to the diocese or country in which they were to be used. English Hours were written according to the Use of Sarum (Salisbury), regardless of where they were made, and differed from those produced for the Dutch (Use of Utrecht) or Italian (Use of Rome) market. As the book was not for liturgical use it was not necessary to write the text solely in Latin. Many were either wholly or partly written in the vernacular.

Books of Hours were produced and read into the sixteenth century, and are one of the manifestations of popular piety in England on the eve of the Reformation. The popularity of Books of Hours, however, made some contribution to the demise of devotional books and of illuminated manuscripts in general. Having promoted literacy among an increasing proportion of the population, and provided reading material in English, some of those readers were stimulated to think and read more widely, exposing them to the radical literature that would undermine the traditional religion of the Middle Ages.

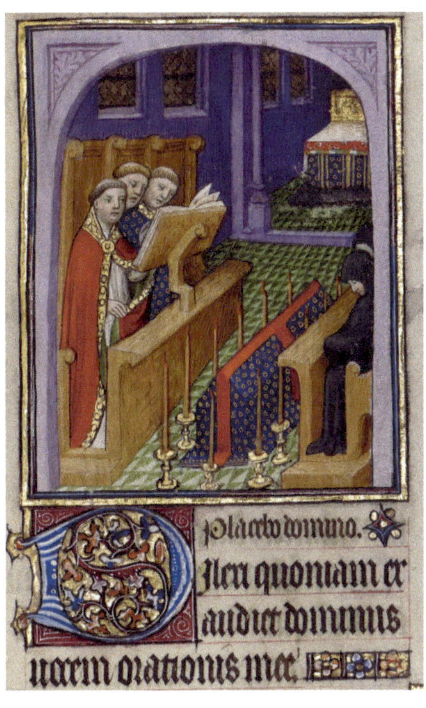

The office of the dead in a fifteenth-century Book of Hours is illustrated with a funeral service.

SECULAR LITERATURE

The idea of a separation between secular and religious literature is a modern idea and not a medieval one, but there were several kinds of books not associated with the Bible, prayer or liturgy that were illustrated. History, science, medicine, travel, philosophy and romance could all have a religious context, just as the calendar was based around religious dates. The Middle Ages was open to wider influences, however, incorporating Arabic science and classical philosophy into its

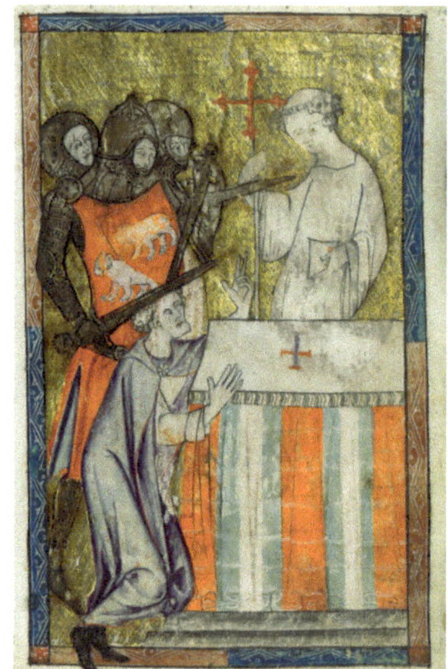

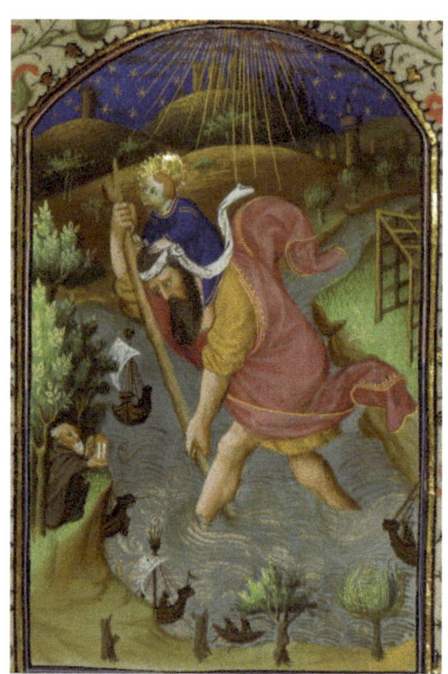

libraries of illuminated manuscripts. Only a small proportion of what we now know of classical literature was known in the Middle Ages, which included works such as Virgil's *Aeneid* and Aesop's Fables.

The Bestiary, or book of beasts, was not a book of Christian observance containing prayers or Bible extracts, but it crossed the boundary between secular and religious, and between medieval and classical. Bestiaries were especially popular in England in the twelfth and thirteenth centuries, but were not a work of natural history as we would understand it. The world and the creatures that lived in it comprised a moral universe in which anything that breathed expressed some aspect of the divine order. The purpose of the book was to read in the actions of the animal world lessons for the conduct of humanity. The book therefore combined observations of animals with allegorical tales that revealed their virtues and vices. It was drawn largely from a Greek work known as the *Physiologus*, compiled between the second and fifth centuries AD, via a sixth-century encyclopedia known as the *Etymologiae*, by Archbishop Isidore of Seville.

The subject matter of the Bestiaries offered plenty of opportunities for miniatures. In fact, without its illustrations a Bestiary would be much the poorer. It began with an account of the creation, then proceeded to describe a mix of creatures in turn mythical (like the basilisk and manticore),

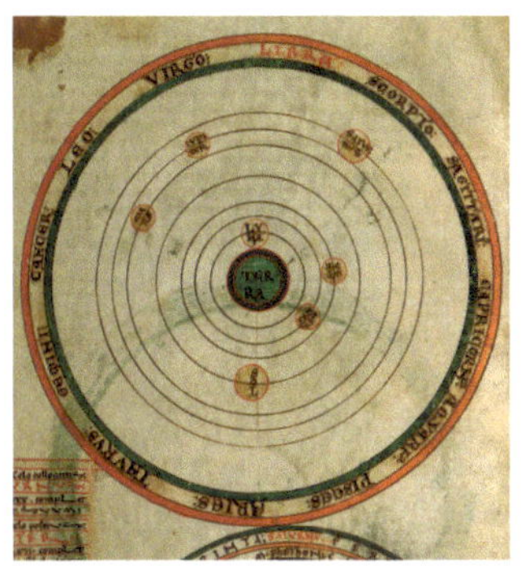

The circle was the favoured means by which to convey scientific or cosmological information in the Middle Ages. In this image from a twelfth-century English Cosmography, written for monks, the Earth is at the centre surrounded by the seven heavenly bodies – Moon, Mercury, Venus, Sun, Mars, Jupiter and Saturn.

exotic and real – although the artists had never seen them (crocodiles and tigers) – and animals that were familiar to everyone (cats, hedgehogs and magpies). Some of the more familiar creatures had not appeared in the earlier Greek texts and were introduced incrementally by a variety of authors. Gerald of Wales described barnacles, geese and ospreys on his journey to Ireland in the twelfth century and they duly began to appear in thirteenth-century English Bestiaries with their characteristic behaviour explained in moral terms.

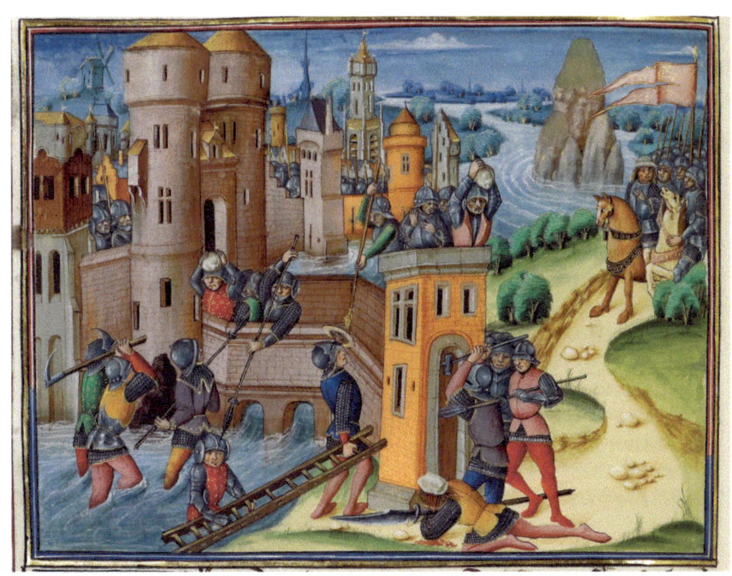

Jean Froissart's *Chronicles* was a history of the Hundred Years' War. This version, produced in Bruges in the 1480s and possibly commissioned by Edward IV, has illustrations tailored for an English reader. Here John of Gaunt attacks St Malo in 1378.

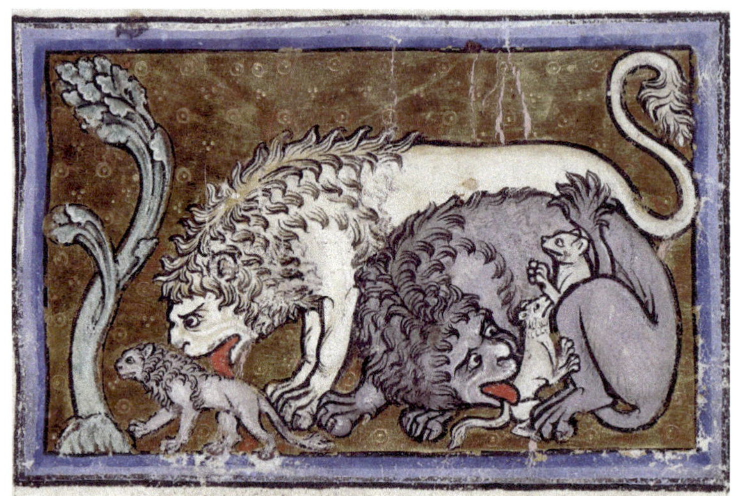

The Bestiary depiction of lions illustrates the myth that a lioness gives birth to still-born cubs who are awakened to life when their father breathes in their faces, just as God awoke Jesus from the dead after three days.

The miniatures in the Bestiaries influenced much of medieval art such as heraldry and carvings in churches, where the dragons, owls and pelicans all have Bestiary origins.

Some of the attributes of these creatures now seem incredible. When hunted, the beaver cut off his testicles and threw them at his pursuer, just as a man should live according to God's commandments and cut off all his vices and shameless deeds in defiance of the devil. The (Indian) elephant with a howdah on its back stoops to take up its burden, just as Jesus humbled himself to raise mankind up. Imaginary creatures generally have sinful associations in the Bestiary. The basilisk was an evil bird that could kill a man by looking at him and poison the water wherever he drinks, but his nemesis was the humble weasel, showing that evil can always be conquered by the faithful soldier of Christ.

The impact of Bestiaries began to decline in the

This image from a Bestiary made in Northumberland c.1250–60 shows a tigress. The hunter has stolen her cubs and thrown down a mirror, which fools the tigress into thinking she has found her cubs. By such means the hunter escapes and the tigress is betrayed by the intensity of her motherly love.

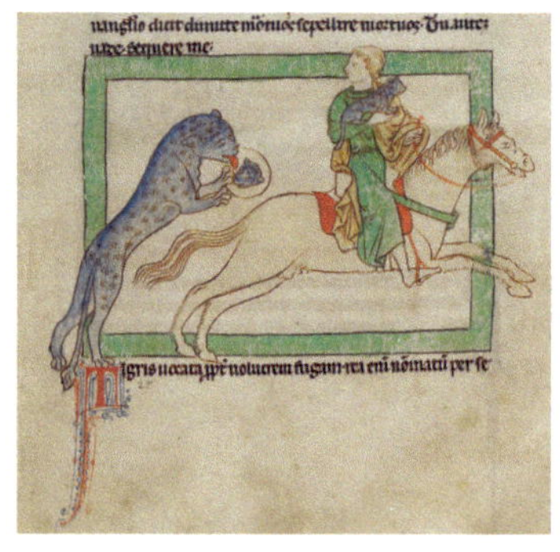

I es ymages et les paintures
D u mur voulentiers remiray
S i vous conterey et diray
D e ces ymages la semblance
S i com moy uient en remenbrance

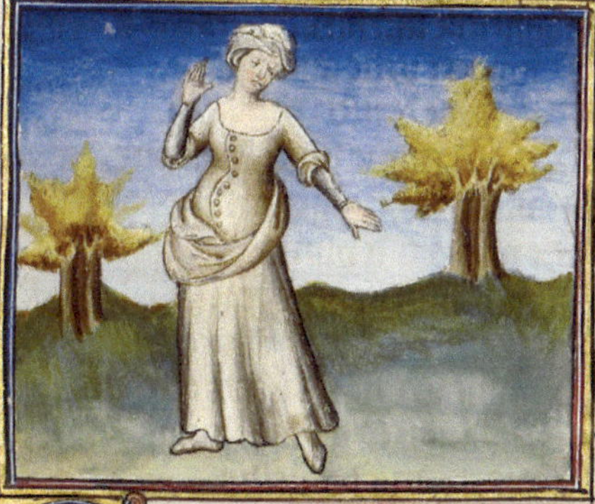

E ns ou milieu ie ui hayne
Q ui de courroux et datayne
S embla bien estre esmouuerresse
E t uenineuse et tancerresse
E t plaine de grant cuuertage
E stoit par semblant cel ymage
S i nestoit pas bien atournee
A ins sembloit estre forcenee
R echignie auoit et froncie
L e uis et le nez secourtie
L edement iert appareillie
C ar elle estoit entourtillie
H ideusement dune touaille
F elonnie. ij.

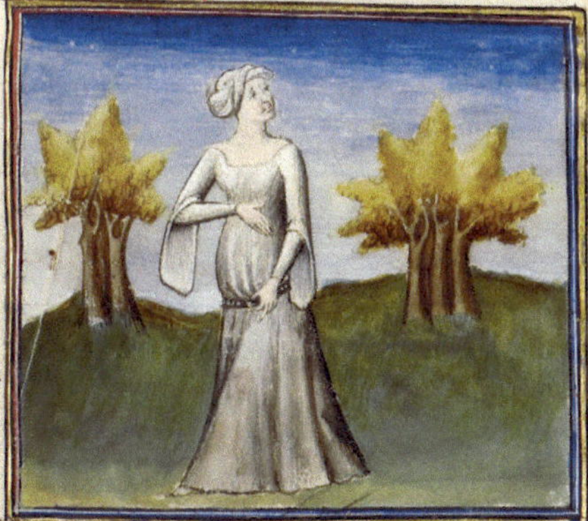

U ne autre ymage dautel taille

A senestre auoit deles lui
S on nom dessus sa teste lui
A preller estoit felonnie Vilenie. iij.

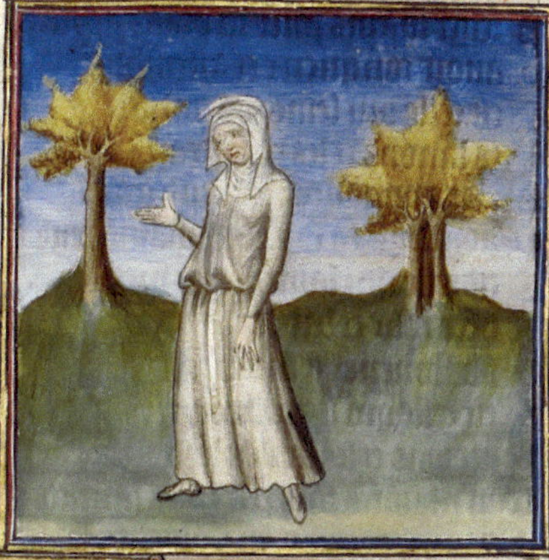

U ne ymage qui uillenie
A uoit nom reui deuers destre
E t estoit auques de tel estre
C om ces deux et dautel faiture
B ien sembloit male creature
E t despiteuse et outrageuse
E t mesdisant et ramponneuse
M oult scot bien faire et bien pourtrare
C ilz qui tel ymage scot faire
C ar bien sembloit estre uillaine
D e douleur et de despit plaine
E t femme qui petit sceust
D onnourer ce quelle deust
C ouuoitise. iiij.

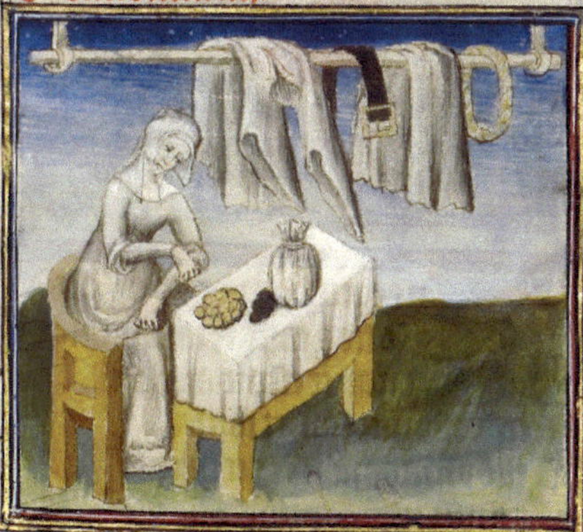

A pres fu painte couuoitise
C est celle qui les gens atise

thirteenth century and its creatures began to migrate to the margins of manuscript illuminations, or other forms of art. Dragons appeared in heraldic devices without the moral attributes that they had once possessed.

The thirteenth century brought with it new kinds of secular as well as religious books, from city workshops that did not need to serve a religious market. Illuminated romances were produced for an aristocratic readership. Songs, poems and folk tales were written down in a spirit of encyclopedic learning, of which the German *Carmina Burana* and *Die Niebelungenlied* (inspiration of Wagner's Ring Cycle), and the French *Le Roman de la Rose* are probably the best known. Over 300 manuscripts survive of the French poem *Le Roman de la Rose,* an allegorical work about the quest for love in which a lover dreams of a beautiful rose held captive in a castle. Its allegorical characters Courtesy, Youth, Fear and Idleness in turn help or hinder him in his quest for the rose.

But probably the best known of the medieval romances are the tales of King Arthur and the Knights of the Round Table. Arthur became a major cultural figure when he appeared in Geoffrey of Monmouth's *History of the Kings of Britain,* completed *c.*1138. His popularity spread rapidly, inspiring several variations, including the Grail romances in France and *Parzifal* in Germany, that went far beyond anything written by the Welsh authors like Nennius who had described him in the ninth century. Arthurian romances were much more than mere entertainment. They gained a religious dimension when, in the early thirteenth century, they became amalgamated with the age of chivalry and especially with the legend of the Holy Grail and its association with Joseph of Arimathea. A late English manuscript version, written in the second half of the fifteenth century, was *Le Morte d'Arthur,* written by Sir Thomas Malory. It has become the best-known medieval English Arthurian romance simply because in 1485 it was published by William Caxton, marking a new era of the printed word in English.

for li mynaist il direment Et lore respondit vne
dame ala royne et dist dame pour dieu doit il
estre si bon chlr come vous dittes. ouil fet le royne
Car il est detoutes pars extraitz du plus bon
chlr du monde et du plus hault lygnage que on
sache Atant descendirent les dames et alerent
oir vespres pour la haultesse du jour Et
quant le roy fut issus du moustier et il vint
au palais en hault si comanda q les nappes
fussent mises Et lore sallerent seoir les com
paignons chm en son lieu ainsi come ilz auo
ient fait au matin Et quat ilz se furent to[us]
assis. lore oyrent vng estoy detonnaire si
grant et si merveilleur quil leur su aduis q

le palais deust fondre Et maintenen entre leur
vng ray desouleil plus cler arent doubles quil
nyauoit denant Si furent tantost par leans
aussi come sils fussent enluminies par lagte
du sant esperit Et comencerent a regarder
lun lautre Car ilz ne savoient dont telle clarte
leur estoit venue Et ny ot cellui qui peust par
leu ne dire mot tant furent menz grans et
petiz Et quat demonves furet crant piece en
telle maniere que nul deulx nauoit pouoir de
parler ainz regardoient tous toe bestes mues

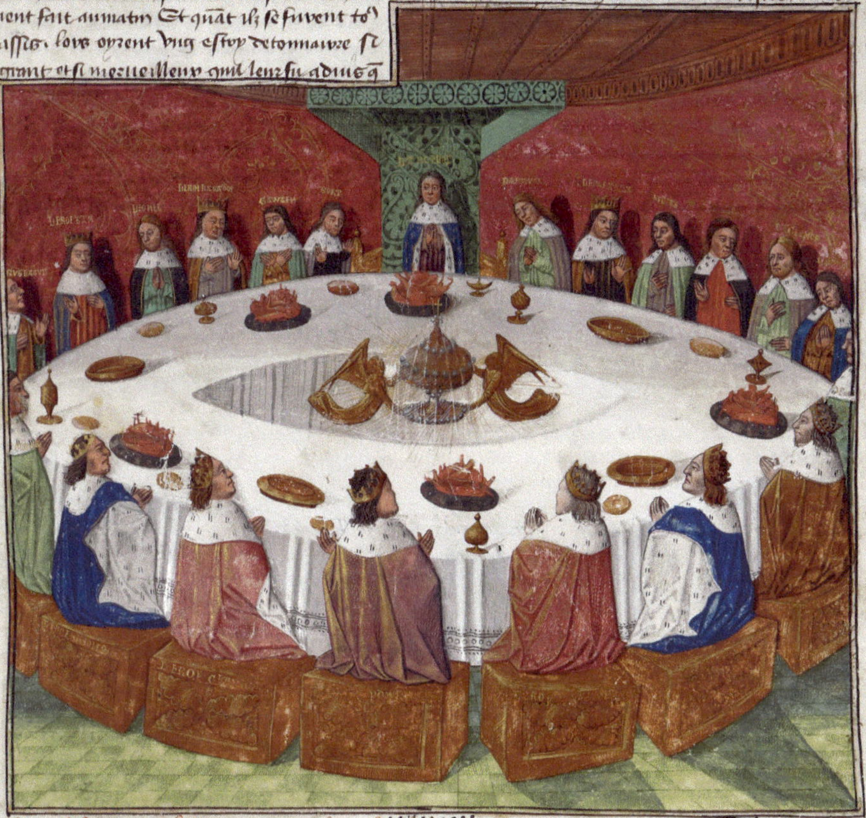

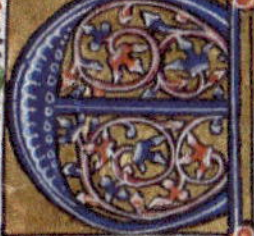

Comt le sant graal sapparut aux chlr de la
table ronde couuert duy blac samyt z ny

[P]ors entra leans z le sang graal
couuert dun blant samit Mais
Il ny eust onques tellui qui
peust voir qui la portoit Si y
entra parmy legrnt huys du palais

eust cellm qui peut apperuoir q le portoit z les
parfu de toutes viandes qlz seruot demader

[E]t maintenant quil ysoit entrec
fut le palais rumply desi bonnes
odeurs que se toutes les espices
du monde y feussent entrees et
espandues Et il ala tout entour

Incipit liber bresith que[m] nos genesim dicimus

In principio creauit deus celu[m] et terram. Terra autem erat inanis et vacua: et tenebre erat sup facie abissi. et sps dni ferebat sup aquas. Dixitq; deus. Fiat lux. Et facta e lux. Et vidit deus lucem cp esset bona: z diuisit luce a tenebris. appellauitq; lucem diem z tenebras nocte. Factuq; est vespe et mane dies unus. Dixit cp deus. Fiat firmamentu in medio aquaz: z diuidat aquas ab aquis. Et fecit deus firmamentu: diuisitq; aquas que erat sub firmamento ab hijs q erat sup firmamentu. et factu e ita. Vocauitq; deus firmamentu celu: z factu e vespe et mane dies secud9. Dixit vero deus. Congregent aque que sub celo sut in locu unu z appareat arida. Et factu e ita. Et vocauit deus aridam terra: congregacionesq; aquaz appellauit maria. Et vidit deus cp esset bonu. et ait. Germinet terra herba virentem et facientem semen: z lignu pomifez faciens fructu iuxta genus suu: cui9 semen in semetipo sit sup terra. Et factu e ita. Et protulit terra herba virente z faciente seme iuxta genus suu: lignuq; faciens fructu z habes unuqdq; semente scdm specie sua. Et vidit deus cp esset bonu: et factu est vespe et mane dies tercius. Dixitq; aute deus. Fiant luminaria in firmameto celi: z diuidat diem ac nocte: z sint in signa z tpa et dies z annos: ut luceat in firmameto celi et illuminet terra. Et factu e ita. Fecitq; deus duo luminaria magna: lumiare maius ut pesset diei et lumiare min9 ut pesset nocti z stellas: z posuit eas in firmameto celi ut lucerent sup terra: et

pessent diei ac nocti: z diuiderent luce ac tenebras. Et vidit de9 cp esset bonu: et factu e vespe z mane dies quartus. Dixit etia de9. Producat aque reptile anime viuentis z volatile super terra sub firmameto celi. Creauitq; deus cete grandia. et omne aiam viuente atq; motabile qua pduxerat aque i species suas: z omne volatile scdm gen9 suu. Et vidit deus cp esset bonu: benedixitq; eis dicens. Crescite z mltiplicamini: z replete aquas maris: auesq; mltiplicent sup terra. Et factu e vespe z mane dies quitus. Dixit quoq; deus. Producat terra aiam viuente in gen3 suo: iumenta z reptilia: z bestias terre scdm species suas. Factuq; e ita. Et fecit de9 bestias terre iuxta species suas: iumenta z omne reptile terre i genere suo. Et vidit deus cp esset bonu: et ait. Faciamus hoiem ad ymagine z silitudine nostra: z presit piscib9 maris: et volatilib9 celi z bestijs uniuseq; terre: omiq; reptili qd mouetur i terra. Et creauit deus hoiem ad ymagine z silitudine sua: ad ymagine dei creauit illu: masculu z femina creauit eos. Benedixitq; illis deus: z ait. Crescite z mltiplicamini z replete terra: et sbicite ea: et dnamini piscib9 maris: et volatilib9 celi et uniuersis aniatib9 que mouet sup terra. Dixitq; de9. Ecce dedi vobis omne herba afferente semen sup terra: et uniusa ligna que hut in semetipis semete genis sui: ut sint vobis i esca z cunctis aiantib9 terre: oniq; voluc celi z uniuersis q mouetur in terra: z i quib3 est anima viues: ut habeat ad vescendu. Et factu est ita. Viditq; deus cunta que fecerat: z erat valde bona.

THE PRINTING PRESS AND REFORMATION

IN THE EARLY 1450s Johann Gutenberg, working in Mainz in the Rhineland of Germany, issued the first printed edition of the Bible, the famous 42-line Bible. It was the first significant product of the printing press, but otherwise was not a radical book – it was still the Latin Vulgate translation and it looked like a manuscript because it was written in a Gothic script in two columns. Gutenberg's Bibles included illuminations, but copies were evidently sent out from the printing press for decoration by hand at the discretion of the customer, so they were still personalised in this early phase. The copy at Lambeth Palace in the possession of the Church of England was printed in Germany but illuminated in London.

In the long run the printing press had a clear advantage over the scriptoria of Europe's cities. Although it was expensive to set the type for a book, once it had been completed then multiple copies could be printed cheaply and quickly. Some of these first Bibles were printed on vellum, but the majority of surviving examples are printed on paper. Paper is quicker and easier to mass produce than vellum, which also helped the printed book become the medium for a mass audience.

William Caxton set up his printing press in Westminster in 1476 and, after his death in 1491, his assistant Wynkyn de Worde (died *c*.1534), a Dutch immigrant, was the first to set up business in Fleet Street, which for four centuries

The Gutenberg Bible is printed with a Gothic typeface but in this edition the opening of the Book of Genesis has been hand illuminated.

was the most famous centre of the printed word. Publishers concentrated on subjects for which there would be a market, simply because they had to sell multiple copies of the product. Gutenberg's Bibles served a healthy market for large Bibles for reading in church services in Germany. Over time that changed, however. Printing presses needed authors, and so many of the manuscripts delivered to the publishers for printing were works of radical theology. The printing press allowed the quick and cheap dissemination of new ideas, including works by scholars and radicals who rejected the fundamental teachings of the Roman Catholic Church. The Protestant Reformation which swept through Europe in the sixteenth century, covering Germany, Switzerland, England, Wales and Scotland, was aided by the availability of books. Without the printing press Henry VIII would have been unable to order in 1538 that every parish church should have a copy of the Bible in English.

Whereas manuscripts were hand illustrated, it became possible to illustrate printed texts with woodcut illustrations. Many leading artists of the sixteenth century were involved in this kind of work, including Albrecht Dürer (1471–1528) and Pieter Breughel the Elder (1525–69). Fashions in art also changed. Panel painting in oil achieved an equal status with miniature painting by the end of the fifteenth century. The acknowledged last great miniature painter was the Flemish artist Simon Bening (c.1483–1561). His calendar miniatures display a clear similarity with the landscape paintings of the next generation of panel painters. The fortunes of the Bening family tell us much about how the world of the professional artist was changing through the generations. A self-portrait by Simon Bening is one of the early examples of a new artistic genre, the 'portrait miniature', which was especially popular in Elizabethan England and was not bound into a book. Simon Bening's father, Alexander Bening (died 1519), was a miniaturist working on illuminated manuscripts in Ghent but Simon's daughter, Livinia Teerlinc (died 1576), was court painter in England to the Tudor monarchs from Henry VIII to Elizabeth, and specialised in portrait miniatures.

The Reformation that began in the 1530s under Henry VIII had a profound impact on the survival of medieval manuscripts. The monasteries were dissolved between 1536 and 1539, and the divine office was no longer sung. All of the monasteries' possessions, including books, were surrendered to the crown and most were destroyed. After Edward VI became king in 1547 there were more profound changes to the liturgy. Prayers for the dead were abolished and the concept of purgatory was declared an error, all of which undermined traditional Catholic Christianity. Then the Mass was abolished in favour of the Protestant Eucharist, and services were no longer conducted in Latin but in English, using the new Book of Common Prayer published in 1549. Parishes were ordered to dispose of their old books, including Missals and Psalters, and, although the majority of them were utilitarian and sparsely decorated, the loss of medieval illuminated manuscripts in this period was significant.

The church did not throw everything away, however, and many beautiful books were in private hands. Illuminated manuscripts were shelved in libraries and often escaped Protestant iconoclasts if they belonged, for example, to the cathedrals rather than the monasteries. Hereford Cathedral has retained over 200 medieval manuscripts. In closed volumes the images were sheltered from the light and so are usually in excellent condition. After all the destruction of the Reformation, books have survived much better than other forms of art like wall painting, sculpture or embroidery. Over 250 books produced at St Augustine's Abbey in Canterbury have survived, but the abbey itself has been in ruins since the Reformation.

Care of old books began early. Queen Elizabeth assumed the throne in 1558 and appointed a new Archbishop of Canterbury, Matthew Parker. He commandeered about 600 early manuscripts that had been confiscated from cathedrals and salvaged from the dissolved monasteries. Many of these made their way to Cambridge University, including the sixth-century Bible associated with the mission to England ordered by Pope Gregory. The rescue of the majority of British and European illuminated manuscripts, however, was the work of a disparate group of antiquarian collectors, the most common factor between them being that they had money. The great collections in the world's libraries and museums in London, Paris, Munich and New York are mostly the bequests of these collectors.

Sir Thomas Bodley's collection formed the core of the Bodleian Library in Oxford, which opened in 1602. The British Library's collections of manuscripts rely heavily on the libraries of early collectors, like Sir Robert Cotton (1571–1631) and the first and second Earls of Oxford who founded the Harley library in 1704 and purchased manuscripts from across Europe. As book production and distribution was an international business in the Middle Ages, so the collection of books in recent centuries has also been an international phenomenon. There are major collections in the European national institutions and in major international libraries and museums, including several in the USA. Book collecting became fashionable in the nineteenth century and the people with the resources to invest in them had generally made their money in trade and industry. J.P. Morgan (1837–1913) was America's foremost banker in his day, but also a Europhile and avid collector of manuscripts, paintings and other objects, which form the core of what is now the Morgan Library and Museum, founded in New York in 1924. William T. Walters (1820–94) moved to Paris to escape the American Civil War and began a collection that was continued by his son Henry (1848–1931), and is now a major dedicated museum in Baltimore. Over 500 manuscripts collected by the Hart family of Lancashire, who had made their living as rope-makers, were

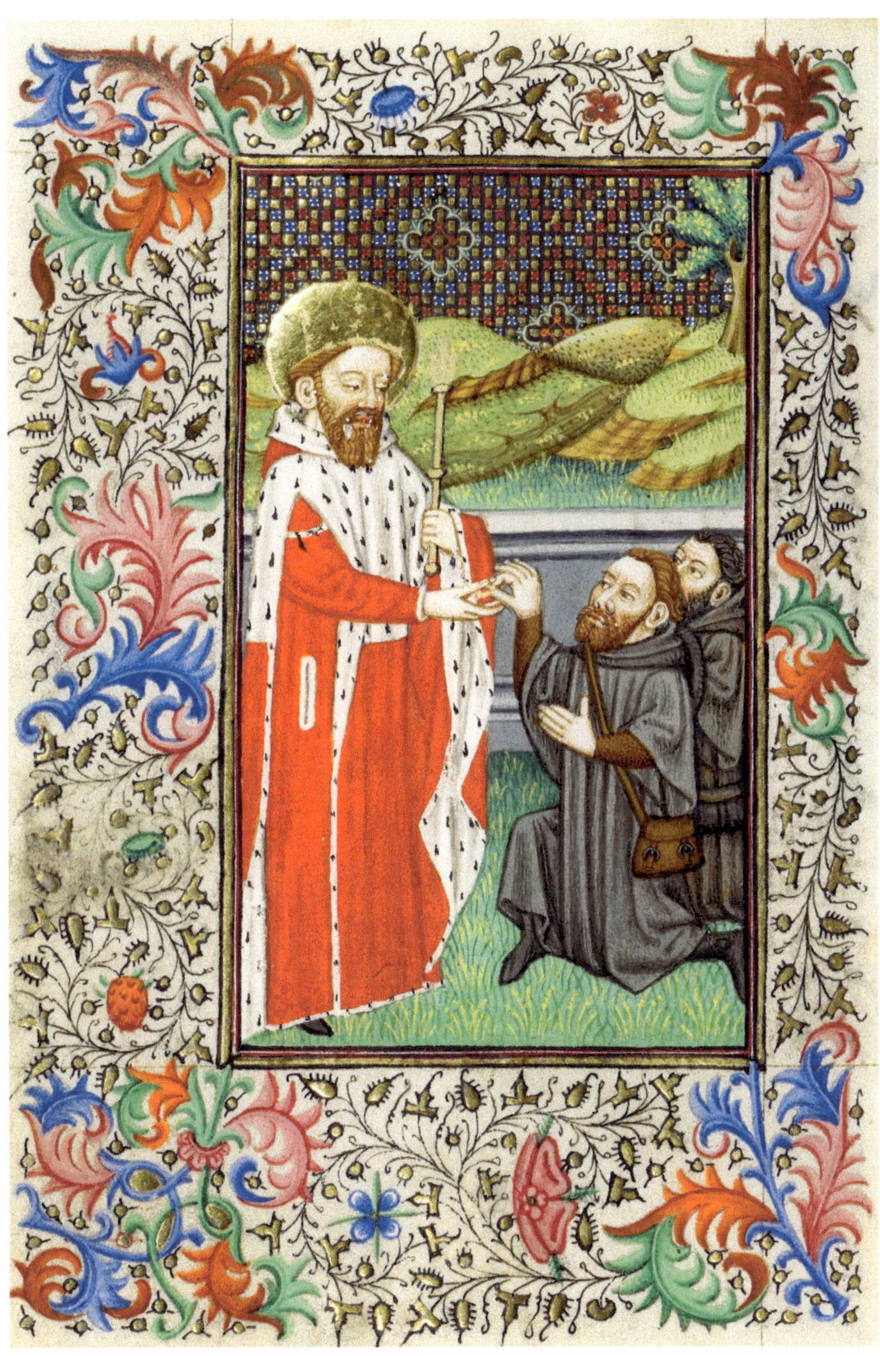

The temptation of Eve and the expulsion from the Garden of Eden is illuminated in the Carrow Psalter, made in East Anglia in the mid-thirteenth century. It had several English owners after the Reformation, and was sold for £4,100 at auction in 1920, just before it was acquired by Henry Walters of Baltimore.

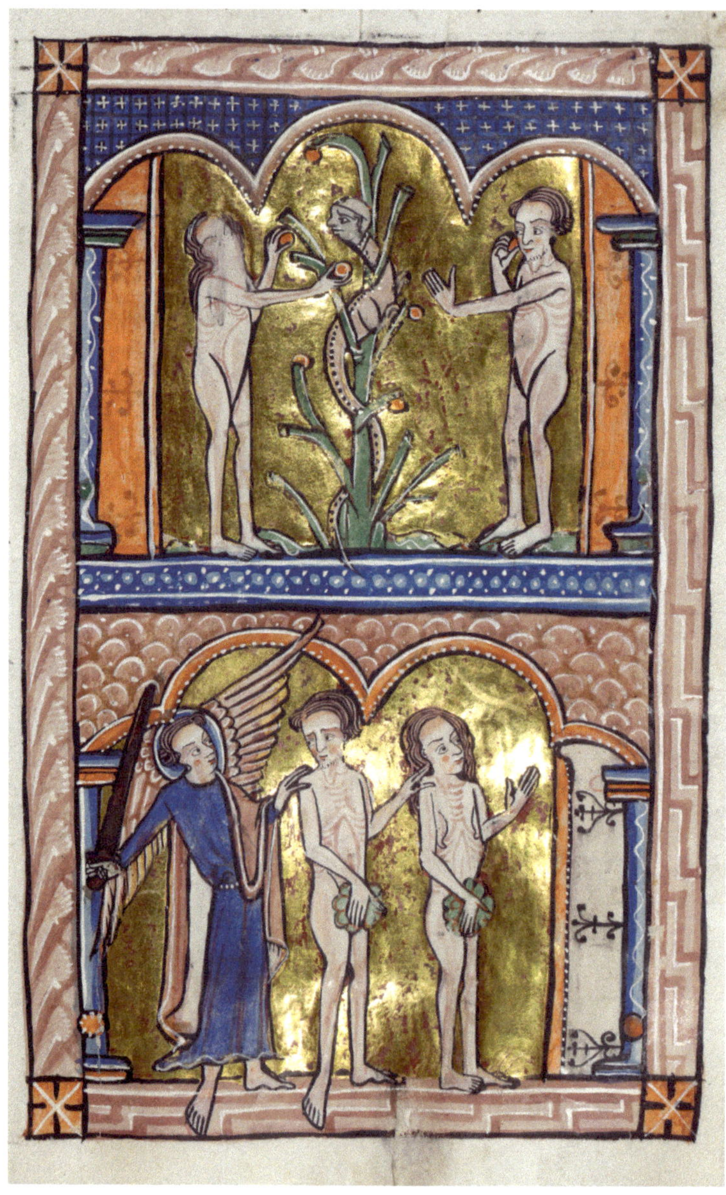

given to the town of Blackburn in 1946. It reminds us that the heritage of the Middle Ages was often saved by grandees of the Industrial Revolution.

PLACES TO VISIT

Blackburn Museum and Art Gallery, Museum Street,
Blackburn BB1 7AJ. Telephone: 01254 667130.
Website: www.blackburnmuseum.org.uk
British Library, 96 Euston Road, London NW1 2DB.
Telephone 01937 546546.
Website: www.bl.uk/events/treasures-of-the-british-library.
A selection of manuscripts is displayed in the Treasures of
the British Library Exhibition.
Durham Cathedral, Durham DH1 3EH.
Telephone: 0191 386 4266.
Website: www.durhamcathedral.co.uk. Some of the
Cathedral's manuscript collection is displayed in the
rolling programme of exhibitions in its 'Open Treasure'
visitor experience.
The Fitzwilliam Museum, Trumpington Street, Cambridge
CB2 1RB. Telephone: 01223 332900.
Website: www.fitzmuseum.cam.ac.uk
Hereford Cathedral Library, Cathedral Close, Hereford
HR1 2NG. Telephone: 01432 374200.
Website: www.herefordcathedral.org
Ranworth Parish Church, Norwich NR13 6HS.
A fifteenth-century Antiphoner is on
display in the church.
Victoria & Albert Museum, Cromwell Road,
London SW7 2RL. Telephone: 020 7942 2000.
Website: www.vam.ac.uk

FURTHER READING

Brown, Michelle. *The Lindisfarne Gospels and the Early Medieval World*. British Library, 2010.

De Hamel, Christopher. *A History of Illuminated Manuscripts*. Phaidon, second edition 1994.

De Hamel, Christopher. *Meetings with Remarkable Manuscripts*. Allen Lane, 2016.

Duffy, Eamon. *Marking the Hours: English people People and Their Prayers, 1240–1570*. Yale University Press, 2011.

Geddes, Jane. *The St Albans Psalter: A Book for Christina of Markyate*. British Library, 2005.

Kerrigan, Michael. *Illuminated Manuscripts: Masterpieces of Art*. Flame Tree Publishing, 2014.

McKendrick, Scot and Doyle, Kathleen. *The Art of the Bible: Illuminated Manuscripts from the Medieval World*. Thames and Hudson, 2016.

Meehan, Bernard. *The Book of Kells*. Thames and Hudson, 2012.

Watson, Rowan. *Illuminated Manuscripts and Their Makers*. V & A Publications, 2003.

ONLINE SOURCES

www.abdn.ac.uk/stalbanspsalter/english/ (St Albans Psalter)

www.bl.uk/manuscripts/ (digitised manuscripts in the British Library)

www.bl.uk/catalogues/illuminatedmanuscripts/GlossA.asp (The British Library glossary of illuminated manuscripts)

www.digital.bodleian.ox.ac.uk (Bodleian Library, Oxford)

www.bsb-muenchen.de/en/collections/manuscripts/search (Bavarian State Library, Munich, Germany)

www.digital.slv.vic.gov.au (State Library, Victoria, Australia)

www.thedigitalwalters.orb/01_ACCESS_WALTERS_MANUSCRIPTS.html (Walters Art Museum, Baltimore, Maryland, USA)

www.library.leeds.ac.uk/special-collections/view/830/
    medieval_illuminated_manuscripts_digital_resource
    (Leeds University Special Collections)
www.lichfield.ou.edu (online images of the St Chad Gospels
    in Lichfield Cathedral)
www.digitalcollections.tcd.ie/home (digital collection of
    manuscripts in Trinity College Library, Dublin, including
    the Book of Kells)
www.digital-scriptorium.org (images from various
    collections held by universities in the USA)
www.metmuseum.org/art/collection (Metropolitan Museum
    of Art, New York, USA)
www.themorgan.org/collection/
    medieval-and-renaissance-manuscripts (The Morgan
    Library & Museum, New York, USA)
www.getty.edu/art/collection (The J. Paul Getty Museum,
    Los Angeles, USA)

Candlemas depicts February in this sixteenth-century calendar illumination by Simon Bening, which is similar to the style of contemporary landscape paintings in oil.

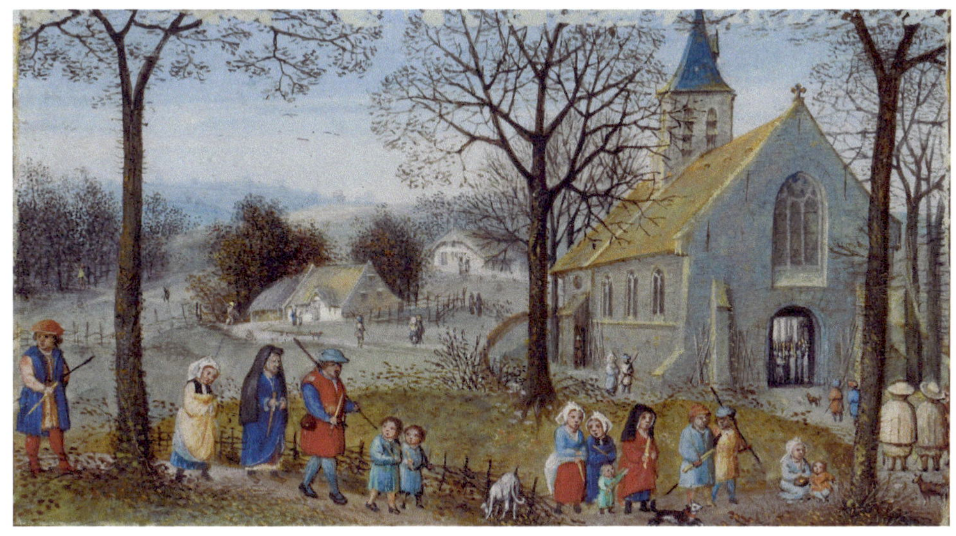

INDEX